A SPIRITUAL JOURNAL
OF HOLISTIC HEALING
FROM A ~ Z

Love + Blessings

Christine Dobyn

A SPIRITUAL JOURNAL
OF HOLISTIC HEALING
FROM A ~ Z

Christine Dobyna

BALBOA.
PRESS

A DIVISION OF HAY HOUSE

Balboa Press books may be ordered through booksellers or by contacting:

Balboa Press
A Division of Hay House
1663 Liberty Drive
Bloomington, IN 47403
www.balboapress.com
1-(877) 407-4847

ISBN: 978-1-4525-4592-9 (sc)
ISBN: 978-1-4525-4591-2 (e)

Because of the dynamic nature of the Internet, any web addresses or links contained in this book may have changed since publication and may no longer be valid. The views expressed in this work are solely those of the author and do not necessarily reflect the views of the publisher, and the publisher hereby disclaims any responsibility for them.

The author of this book does not dispense medical advice or prescribe the use of any technique as a form of treatment for physical, emotional, or medical problems without the advice of a physician, either directly or indirectly. The intent of the author is only to offer information of a general nature to help you in your quest for emotional and spiritual well-being. In the event you use any of the information in this book for yourself, which is your constitutional right, the author and the publisher assume no responsibility for your actions.

Any people depicted in stock imagery provided by Thinkstock are models, and such images are being used for illustrative purposes only.
Certain stock imagery © Thinkstock.

Printed in the United States of America

Balboa Press rev. date: 2/1/2012

I would like to dedicate this book to all those who believed in me and supported me on my journey.

My husband Mark . . . I Love You!
My four wonderful children Kirby, Roslyn, Meagan and Bethany.
My sister Dora and my best friend, without you none of this would have been possible.
My Dad for all his love and showing me how to be strong.
My friend Lorianne, Thank you for the guidance.
And to my Mother who continues to watch over me and keep me in check. I Love You and Miss You!!
Most importantly God . . . Thank You!

INTRODUCTION

This is a journey I never thought I would take. Writing a book, but when you keep getting that nudge from spirit, it's time to take action and move forward. This Journal will give you insight into many different aspects of Holistic Healing, from the emotional, mental, physical and spiritual side of things.

You will be able to connect with some or all of the subjects I have written about throughout this book. You may even find what in your own life needs change. This journal will help you to understand and learn about many new things from A-Z. I cover everything I know from Angels, Affirmations all the way to Zip to it and everything in between.

I know that my purpose in life is to help, heal and guide those who are looking for the true light within. People who want to change the way they think and feel, but may be afraid to or just don't know how. I will tell you right now that it is a journey for everyone. Change is not an easy thing. Some of the topics in this book may be a lot easier to read than to do, but always remember, take one day at a time, never give up and practice, practice, practice.

Change for us is like setting a goal. You need to figure out what it is you want, and then go after them one at a time. Always have faith and trust in God, that he/she wants good for all of us. I choose God because that is my belief. Many believe in someone or something else and that is fine. So whenever I mention God feel free to put in who or what your belief is, such as the Universe, the Creator, or what have you. This book has no reference to any certain religion, but is written on a Spiritual level.

As for myself, I am Catholic. I no longer practice anymore, but some of my views come from the church, such as Angels, which are in many different religions and belief systems. I also believe in Jesus, Mother Mary and other spiritual subjects. So today I consider myself spiritual only and do not attend any church. So please feel free to take what you want from this book and leave the rest behind. The only things that I ask is that you remain open to all that you read in this book. It just may make sense to you. If anything at least try any and all things you will read about. As I always say "I'll try anything once". It can't hurt. So please be open, try something new and if it doesn't resonate with you, let it go.

Have you ever looked at your life and said "why me"? Many of you including myself have been there, sometimes more than once. There are times in life when things go wrong for us and we wonder how did things go so wrong? Many times we create what happens in our lives through our thoughts without realizing we are creating this bad time in our lives.

Other situations that we go through are life lessons that we contracted for ourselves when we decided we were coming here. We go through these lessons for our spiritual growth. Look back at some of the tough times you have had in life and think to yourself, what did I learn from that? We learn from every experience we go through in our lives. Maybe you have learned to stand up for yourself, how to let go, how to forgive, how to release anger or set boundaries. Everything has good and bad. The most important thing is to let go of the bad and take what you have learned from the good. Life is only as good or bad as you make it, so choose and decide, how do you want your life to be? Do you want to be the victim or the victor?

I have been through many situations in life, just like all of you. I have learned over the years that I can make anything better. Just by changing my perception. It didn't happen overnight, believe me. In fact things didn't start changing for me in a spiritual way until I was 28 years old. At that time in my life I was married and the marriage was falling apart, but I was in denial. I didn't see any of it. I was wearing blinders. My belief at that time was, you got married and stayed married. That is what the church taught me. I soon realized that it didn't feel right to me. Did God expect me to stay with someone even though neither one of us was happy? I didn't think so anymore.

One day my Mother called me and told me to put on the TV. There was this guy who was a medium and I needed to see him. Well I was blown away by what he was saying. Not only his messages to callers but also his spiritual message to everyone who was listening. He was promoting his new book and you know what? Next day I was out there buying it. I started to read this book and t was like the floodgates opened up for me.

Now I have always had the belief in intuition and spirit, but I had never seeked out information on it or even tried to practice it. When I was a child I could connect with spirit so easily. I remember seeing and hearing spirit all the time. I had no idea though what it all meant. One day I asked my mother what it meant when people heard voices in their head. She told me they must be crazy. Well I shut that off in a hurry, I didn't want anyone thinking I was some crazy person. You see my mother was psychic and she did know what I was talking about, but did not want me to have the same ability. I was only 7 years old. Mom was shown things she didn't like and didn't want me to see the same things. Of course back in the 1970's psychics were not heard of a lot and there were not any classes on how to control your abilities. Unlike today, you can take many classes to learn how to connect with spirit and know how to control what you are shown in a message.

As I became a teenager I was very interested in psychics and getting readings. It was then that my mother told me she was intuitive. I then told her I wanted to be intuitive too and she said no and explained to me that being psychic was not a gift I wanted. So I left it alone, but still went to psychic readers for guidance.

Now back to when my mother introduced me to this medium that was on TV. I was 28 years old. I continued to read more books and learned a lot more. At this time my marriage was getting worse. I started to get signs from spirit. My wedding photo would be found on the floor face down, when it have never fallen before. My Grandfather who had passed a few years before started making himself know by appearing to me three times, a full body manifestation. I thought that was the greatest thing ever to see a spirit, but in all reality it was a warning that things were falling apart and my husband was about to leave me. Well sure enough not long after my husband at the time did walk out. I was devastated and wondered why. Not long after I did see what was really going on. I had removed the blinders and saw the truth and it was the best thing that could have happened to me. Today I am re-married to a wonderful man and have a son, set of twin girls and a beautiful stepdaughter.

I continued to read more books and take in as much information as I could. I was beginning to open up intuitively. While dating my present husband, I had seen his father who had passed away four years before. When I asked him what his Dad looked like and described him to a tee,

I think I freaked him out a little. He was so shocked and asked me how I knew that, I told him that I saw him and was standing right next to me. I had shocked myself as well. It was then I knew that I had to continue to learn and connect.

As I learned more and more, my ability became stronger. I was getting more signs and trusting what I was feeling, even though my ego would get in the way at times and make me doubt myself. It was at this time that I was invited to a psychic medium home party with my sister Dora. This is where the medium looked at both of us and said that we would be opening our own business together. We were like, what? At the time I was a stay at home Mom and my sister worked for Polaroid, so what could we possibly do that we both had an interest in? The woman proceeded to say that Dora would be doing Massage Therapy and I would be doing Reiki and Hypnotherapy. Well I had no idea what Reiki was, never mind do it. I heard of Hypnotherapy but didn't think I would be doing it.

Now I was so curious as to what Reiki was that I went to the bookstore the next day and bought a book about it. I read it from cover to cover in one day and right then and there I knew Reiki is what I wanted and felt it in my heart. I called the woman who gave us the reading and asked her where I could go to learn Reiki. She gave me a name of a great teacher and I was on my way to my Holistic Career. At the same time Dora started her search for a Massage School.

In May 2005 I became a Reiki I Practitioner, August 2005 I went for my Reiki II, February 2006 I was certified in Hypnotherapy and Dora finished school in January 2006. After the holidays in 2005 we started looking for a place to start our center and with the guidance of the Angels, we found THE place. On March 1, 2006, Sisters Of Solace—Holistic Healing Center was started. We opened without any cliental, but knew that this was meant for us. So we trusted that God would send us the people and oh my gosh, did he.

It is now 2011 and after five years in business we have grown so much. We offer so many more modalities than we did five years ago and now have classes and events. I became a Reiki III Master/Teacher, Angel Therapy Practitioner/Angel Card Reader, Theta Master, Ear Candler, IET (Intergraded Energy Therapy), Chakra Balancing, Crystal Healings, became a non-denominational Reverend, hold Spiritual Counseling

Group Sessions and I am in the process of practicing Soul Transfiguration (Working with Heavens Light).

Dora is a Licensed Massage Therapist and offers Swedish, deep tissue, Hot stone and Aromatherapy Massage. She also does Reflexology and Ear Candling.

At Sisters Of Solace we also have Meditations, Clarity Breathwork, Spiritual Counseling, Angel Therapy Certification Classes, Reiki Classes and other Practitioners who also work from our center offering Yoga, Qi Gong, Angel Circles, Law of Attraction, Mediumship group events, Tarot readers, and so much more.

I thank God everyday for this opportunity he/she has given me and for every new experience that comes along. I pray that God, the Angels and spirit continue to work with me and guide me along my path of healing, light and happiness and to continue to help all those who seek the same in their own lives.

A—ANGELS

Angels are Heavenly beings sent by God to do his work and help humanity. Angels come in many forms and are of different vibrations. I call upon the Angels everyday in my life. Whether it be for my own personal reasons, my healing work, doing Angel card readings or for guidance while teaching classes or Spiritual Counseling. I have seen the most amazing things happen during these times. During my healing work, they have come into the room when I invoke them. I see them helping me with the healings, with great results that are confirmed by my clients when the session is over. Many times my clients tell of feeling other hands on them when they know my hands are on another part of their body. They also explain to me that they feel a great warmth come over them, which is a sign that the Angels are around. A sense of calmness, pain and emotional issues pulled away from their bodies and at times clients have said that they saw an Angel in their minds eye. Angels are truly beautiful and amazing beings of light.

Another aspect of my work is teaching Angel Certification Classes, where I teach people who the Angels are, how to work with them, who to work with, how to watch for signs, receive messages and do angel card readings for themselves as well as others. Working with the Angels can be for personal use as well as professional. In my opinion everyone should be calling on the Angels for guidance and messages. If you don't know how, then learn.

Many people choose to stay in a bad way, feeling like there is nothing they can do to change things. When in fact change is very possible, if you want it. First you need to choose to change and then call on the Angels for help and guidance. First rule of working with the Angels is that the Angels will not help you unless you ask! They do not interfere in our lives. They do not make decisions for us, why, because we have free will, they can only guide us then it is up to us to make a decision. The Angels will guide us to a positive outcome by signs or messages.

Many of you may be saying that you pray to God, why should you ask the Angels? Well you can pray to God or whomever you pray to. In all reality when you pray to God he sends his Angels to do his work for him. You see, God does not hold a physical form. God is of total loving energy and is of the highest vibration. You can do both, pray to God and ask the Angels for their assistance.

Ascended Masters, Teachers and Saints are also divine beings that you can call upon for guidance. They are beings that did live a life here on earth and continue their work from the other side. Angels on the other hand never lived a life in human form except for Archangel Sandlphon and Archangel Metatron. Guardian Angels can be someone who lived a life, such as a grandparent, sister, brother, and so on. Many times a loved will choose to take the job as your guardian Angel and watch over you for your remainder of time here on earth.

There are many different types of Angels. They are of different levels and vibrations. The higher the level, the higher the vibration. Below you find a list of the levels of Angels:

1. Guardian Angels—Protectors, everyone has one
2. Archangels—Messengers, Helpers
3. Cherubim—Joyous Singers
4. Seraphim—Joyous Singers
5. Powers—Healers
6. Carrions—Carriers of the Dark Entities
7. Virtues—Helpers, Peaceful Warriors
8. Dominions—Overseers of good
9. Thrones—God's army, Pure Love
10. Principalities—God's army, Pure Light, closest to God

All Angels have certain jobs to do. Some work with us here and others only come when God directs them to do so. Such as when we all experienced 9/11. You can be sure that every Angel in heaven was in New York City on that day.

Now as far as I go, I work with the Archangels in my personal life as well as my healing work and readings at my center. I always call upon them for assistance, guidance and messages. Another way I connect with then is to write in my journal and then pick some Angel Cards. Those cards never cease to amaze me. I also ask the Angels for signs and messages, so that I can be clear on whatever decision-making I have. They never tell me what to do, but always give me great guidance as to which way I need to go.

Archangels give us many signs. You have probably seen many signs from them, but passed it off as a coincidence. Think about this for a minute. How many times have you seen repetitive numbers, found feathers, found coins, saw street signs that said something that resonated with you? Have you ever heard a song on the radio and the words just hit home for you, maybe saw a TV commercial that it seemed like the announcer was talking just to you? For example: My sister wanted to start massage school and was still debating on where to go. She needed a class that would accommodate her work schedule. She told me one day while at home she had said to herself, "Where should I go to school"? No sooner did she say that, a commercial came on the TV for a massage school and they were saying, want to be a massage therapist, enroll now. Well she was blown away! She got on the phone and called that school. She was even more shocked to find out that they were taking new students and that there was ONE spot left. The hours they offered even worked out for her. So she was able to go to school in the morning and work at night. So as you can see the Angels have great ways of giving us messages when we ask. So pay attention and you too can pick up the signs.

All you have to do is be open to it. Don't try to hard because then you will block yourself to receiving any messages.

Here is a list of the Archangels. Who they are and a little of what they help us with:

1. Archangel Ariel—protects earth, helps animals, works with the elemental and fairies.
2. Archangel Azrael—Helps newly crossed over souls, helps spiritual teachers
3. Archangel Chamuel—helps find new love, friends, new job, or lost items
4. Archangel Gabriel—assist writers, teachers, journalist, overcoming fear in communication
5. Archangel Haniel—peace, serenity, harmony
6. Archangel Jeremiel—divine wisdom, comfort, emotional healing, forgiveness
7. Archangel Jophiel—helps artist, beauty, feng shui

8. Archangel Metatron—helps children, helps Indigos and crystals on their spiritual path
9. Archangel Michael—removes fears, doubt and things that no longer serve us, protection, strength, and courage
11. Archangel Raguel—justice, balanced power, fairness
12. 11.Archangel Raphael—physical healing, helps healers, traveling
13. Archangel Sandlphon—music, answered prayers, assist Michael
14. Archangel Uriel—problem solving, helps students
15. Archangel Zadkiel—memory, helper of students, intuition

Protection is another service the Angels provide. I call on the Angels daily to protect my home, my car when I'm driving, my husband when he is working (He drive a gas tanker), My children while they are at school and while I am doing healing work or readings. I call on them when I am working with clients because I work with Spirit and do not want to connect with any lower or negative energy.

Negative or lower type energies are something we all deal with on a daily basis. Unfortunately some have to work with those who are very negative or even at times deal with family members who are not of good light. Always ask the Angels, especially Archangel Michael to surround and protect you from these lower and negative energies. He is the protector. Ask that you be surrounded in white light so these negative forces cannot penetrate through.

Other ways to protect yourself is to surround yourself with diamonds, mirrors facing outward to deflect the bad energy back to where it came from and you can also zip up. Zip up means reaching down to your feet and make the motion of pulling up a zipper all the way up to the top of your head. I know your probably saying, yea right, can that really work? Well yes it does and I have shown my students and clients through muscle testing. When protected the muscles are strong and can resist pressure. When not protected the muscles are weak and cannot fight off pressure. We all need to protect ourselves everyday. I do and it has made quite a difference.

So now that you know a little bit more about the Angels, why not start working with them on a regular basis. Still not sure if this is possible. Well then I just ask that you be open to the possibilities. Give it a try! The Angels don't mind being challenged; they love to give us signs. So the next time you go to the store or your local mall, ask the Angels before you leave to give you a clear and safe passage to the store and that you want a parking space right in front of the door. Then watch what happens. I use this all the time . . . . and ALWAYS get a parking space!

Just a note, that if you ask for something and don't get it, know that it may not be the right time and to be patient. The Angels always help and give us what we need, but they also know that timing is everything. So I ask that you just be patient and trust with your heart that they hear you and will help you.

You may be thinking, why should the Angels help me? I don't have a great life, I have made so many mistakes in my life. Truth is that the Angels are beings of pure light and love and NEVER judge us. They help ALL who ask. You may feel like you don't need help or you can do it all on your own. Why not ask for the help? Why struggle? God did not put us on this earth to struggle and be sad. Allow the Angels to help you. They are God's messengers and helpers and God does want us to be happy. We are all here to learn for our spiritual self. We all need to progress our spiritual side by learning from every experience we go through in our lives. Remember no matter how bad things seem, there is always something positive from it and something to learn. Sometimes we just don't see it right away.

To work with the Angels you can choose one from the list on the previous page or just ask in general and the right Angel(s) will assist you with whatever you need. Just tell them your situation, ask for their assistance and guidance as to how to resolve the issue and then just let it go and trust that they are helping you. If you dwell on it and continually ask over and over, you actually block the progress. You are closing yourself to the guidance they are trying to give you because you are only focused on why, why, why and when, when, when. Here is an example: When you go to a restaurant, the wait person takes your order and then you trust that they will give your order to the cook and then will give the food to wait person to bring to you. It is a process. You don't continually ask the waitperson for what you want. You TRUST. Well working with the Angels is the same. Ask for what you need, trust and wait for the signs and messages. You may have to wait a little while for the results but you will get them. I hope this helps you to fully understand.

Working with the Angels can be very uplifting, exciting and wonderful. You deserve to be happy, full of Love and living in a positive way. Let go of the judgment, drama and negative so you can live in a life of peace and harmony.

Here is a meditation that you can use to connect with the Angels. First be sure of what it is you want. Close your eyes. Now take 2-3 deep breaths in through the nose and exhale out your mouth (this helps you to relax quickly). Then ask for what you need. Take sometime to sit quietly and listen or sense anything from the Angels. If you don't get anything right away, don't worry about it. It will come to you.

You can also use this meditation as well: Dearest Archangel _____ I ask that you help me with _____. I ask that this situation to be taken care of and that you guide me to what I can do to improve this. I am open to your guidance and messages. I ask for this for my highest and best and the highest and best for all involved, better that I could ever imagine. Thank you Archangel _____ for helping me now.

Note: Always ask for anything you want or need for your highest and best and the highest and best for all involved, better that you could ever imagine. You do not want to receive anything in an ill way. For example: Don't just ask for a new car. You could get your new car by getting into an accident and your car gets totaled; now you have to get one. If you need more money, don't just say I need money, because you could walk out side and find a quarter. So be sure to be specific about what you want and always for the highest and best. So goes the old saying, be careful what you ask for. Lastly be sure to always show your Gratitude for all you ask for and receive!

Affirmation: I fully trust in my Angels and am open to receiving their guidance.

A—AFFIRMATIONS

Affirmations are positive statements and thoughts that bring positive ness to our awareness. It is a way of changing our negative thoughts about ourselves, a situation or someone else.

You see when someone is negative, it seems that everything about him or her and everything around that person is negative. When you are negative you are living in the ego. We all what to be in a place of love, joy and happiness, coming from the heart. You see thoughts and words are energy and when you think or speak that energy goes out to the universe. Then the universe responds by sending back exactly what we sent out. So if you send out positive you get positive back. You send out negative, you get negative back. The universe does not recognize negative words either. So lets say that you are late for work and you keep thinking that you don't want to be late. All the universe hears is I want to be late so guess what . . . you're going to be late. Instead you should say, I have plenty of time to get to work or I am going to be to work in plenty of time. Those are more positive statements.

You will see that when you start to change the way you speak and think into a more positive way, everything falls into place and works out beautifully. You always want to speak and think in the present moment. Don't use "I will" because that is a future statement. Instead say, "I am". That makes it in the present. Lets say that you want to attract something and you say I will attract this. You won't get it because you have just projected it into the future. Say I am getting this. So you will attract it. It's like when people say tomorrow never comes, it's true because when you wake up in the morning it is today. So stay in the present moment and speak and think of what you want in the present.

If you were to sit back and think of everything you talked about today, how much of it is negative? Wee tend to say a lot of negative things without realizing it. Believe me I am no different. I used to say a lot of negative.

Such as, I can't, I should have, could have and so on. Wow so negative! Today I am very mindful of what I say. I do slip up now and then, but the difference now is I catch myself and correct it right away. We are all human and have an ego, but it is our choice of where we want to be. Positive or negative.

It is a daily practice to live in the positive and be open to the fact that yes we do make mistakes and just move on from them, taking the lesson with you. Recognizing what we say and think is the first step. Once we learn that, then we can move onto changing our words and thoughts. It would be so nice if we could just flip a switch and be positive, but we can't. Our human ego I believe is a part of us that teaches us the most. The ego can be a very nasty monster within us and if we let it take over it's not going to be good. No positive anything in a ego. If you have ever felt judgmental, selfish, angry, placed blame, did the shoula, coulda, woulda game, said I can't or deal in gossip and drama, you are working with your ego. We all have dealt with one or more of these, but now you can recognize it, let it go and move more to the positive. God did give us emotions, but we do with them is our lesson to learn . . . choose wisely!

Here is A List Of Positive Affirmations VS. Negative

Negative—Don't Say This

I Can't Do _____.
I'm Going To Be Late.
I Am Overweight.
I Am Always Sick.
My Life Stinks.
Drama Follows Me.
I Never Have Money.
I Have No Friends.
My Husband is Lazy.
My Kids Never Listen.
My Job Stinks.
No Body Loves Me.

Positive Affirmations—Say This

I can do _____.
I Am On Time.
I Lose Weight Easily.
I Am Healthy.
I Have A Great Life.
I Am Around Positive People.
I Am Financially Abundant.
I Have So Many Friends In My Life.
My Husband Is So Helpful.
My Children Are Well Behaved.
I Have A Job That Fills My Purpose.
I Am Surrounded By Love.

These are just a few examples of changing the way you speak or think. Now you may be saying "well some of those are not negative they are true". The thing is that you can change anything you want in your life. Just by changing the thought process, using positive affirmations and believing it to be truth. Change will occur. Some statements may be true in this moment and they will stay that way as long as you keep speaking and thinking it is true.

When we put it out to the universe that we never have money, the universe responds with, don't give that person money they don't want it. If you start to turn that around to I am financially abundant, the universe responds with, send that person money, they are financially abundant. Use affirmations, they work! As one of my teachers told me . . . Fake It Until You Make It! Believe it is so and it will be.

Ever notice in life how you have been told certain things and you take them as truth. Now time goes by and someone or something brings you new information and this can change your mind. Now you take this new information as truth. It is whatever is in your heart and mind that becomes your reality. So to bring change into your life, change the way you think and speak. You CAN change if you really want to. Like I tell my clients, we all have a choice. You can choose to be unhappy or choose to be happy. Make your choice.

Affirmation: I choose a life that is happy, joyful, loving and full of abundance.

B—BELIEF

Belief is a feeling or statement that you understand to be truth. What do you believe? Well everyone has beliefs and some of us have different beliefs than others. As children we are programmed to believe what ever our parents, teachers and religious leaders tell us. Then what happens, we grow up and we start hearing other information that is different from what we were taught. Now you start to question everything you were told. Truth or belief comes from the heart and you have to go with what feels right in your heart. So you start to go with what you feel is your truth and someone may be right there to knock you down saying that is not right. Now you feel guilty. You cannot let anyone make you feel that way. That just shows that they are speaking from their ego and are not open to a different opinion. I'm sure you have heard the saying "we are all entitled to our own opinion". This is very true and we have to respect what others take in as their truths.

Holistic Healing is another belief. I truly believe in working out illness or dis-ease of physical and emotional issues with holistic healing. I also believe that physical issues are cause by emotional imbalance. Don't you feel that when your emotions are off, you feel it in your body?

Belief is something you have to have in yourself as well. So many believe they are not worth it, they are not good enough; they shouldn't be happy and so on. These are beliefs that need to be changed. They are based from the ego and are negative. Some of those beliefs may have come from your childhood. Maybe someone kept telling you all these bad things and now you take that as truth. No Way! Every single one of you is Worth Everything!!

Other beliefs can come from a past life. You can carry over cell memory from a pasted life into this life. Your cell memory can carry over fears, vows of poverty, illness and so much more. Some people can have no fear at all and then one day from out of nowhere you are completely fearful of something. When this happens it is usually because at the age the fear started is when you had the same fear in your past life. Same goes for unexplained pains. It has been shown through hypnosis that people talk of an injury they sustained in a past life at the time that person is in this life. When they are told that the pain is from the past life and not now and they can let it go. After the session they feel so much better and the pain is gone.

Here is an example of past life memories that have carried over. There is a playground near my home and my husband and I would take our kids there from time to time. They were two and three at the time and we decided to take them to the playground. All three of the kids would play on everything. The slide, swings, see saw, and climb on the platforms. Well none of them ever had an issue with climbing up on the platform until this one day after the girls turned two. Our daughter Roslyn started screaming and crying when we put her on the platform. I couldn't figure out why. She was always up there without an issue. So I took her down and she played on other things. That night when she went to sleep, I softly talked into her ear and told her that what ever happened in her past life is no longer with her and she is in a new life now and there is no need to be fearful. She should just have fun. Everything is ok. We went back to the playground a few days later and she went right up on the platform with no problem and had a great time. What I did was a form of hypnosis and anyone can do this with his or her own kids if they feel that there is a fear that came up out of now where.

Religion is another belief that we are taught as children. We may all follow different religions but it is my belief that we all started with the same belief . . . God! All religions teach different aspects of what happened after God. Having a religious belief is a wonderful thing no matter what you practice, as long as you are happy with it.

As for me, I was raised Catholic. I never felt comfortable in the church for as far back as I can remember. The longer I went to church the more I didn't agree with what I was being told. I found that the rules would change to suit them and they didn't always seem to come from place of love. Here is what I am talking about. Years ago St. Patrick's Day landed on a Friday during lent. Well they decide to change the rules and let people eat meat on that Friday. Well they also taught that if you ate meat on Friday, you would go to hell. As one of my favorite authors, Sylvia Browne said: did they bring back all the people from hell and let them go to heaven because they changed the rules? I just feel that some people from the church can be very judgmental and live in the ego. Now this is my opinion and I am very open to whatever everyone else believes. For me I call myself spiritual. I do believe in God, Jesus, Mary and many other aspects of the religion, just not all the rules and close mindedness.

I truly believe a lot of the teachings out there of any religion are true to a point and the rest is man made. I have heard so many times that the bible says so. Well there are 26 versions of the bible. Which one is the right one? It is true the bible says this and that, but which part came from God and which part was written by man through his own way of interpretation? Now you know as well as I do that when any story is told verbally and carried on from one person to another, the story starts to change. My belief is that the churches put in a lot of what they wanted to benefit them. They also use scare tactics to keep people in church. How many times have we heard that if you don't go to church you will go to Hell? Well there is no such place. This did work for a while, but today more and more people are starting to question their religion and their beliefs. They are looking more into their hearts and what feels right to them. I have met so many people that call themselves spiritual and don't belong to any certain religion.

Remember that these statements are my beliefs and I don't expect anyone to follow what I say. I expect people to go with what feels right to them. You need to look into your heart and say, "what feels right to me"? My wish is for everyone to love everyone and live your life in the eyes of God and your own truths. Never feel guilty either. Many people I have talked to say that if their Mom knew they weren't going to church and were just praying and working with the Angels on their own, She would be so mad. I went through the same thing with my Grandmother. She would be so upset because I wasn't going to church, but I had to do what felt right to me. I can't do something that feels wrong and do it just to make others happy. Follow your heart not your ego. Always look within!

Other subjects that are beliefs are angels, past life lives, reincarnation, physics, mediums, connecting with spirits and so on. I understand are these to be truth. I have connected with angels, spirits, and loved ones. I am very intuitive and have brought people into their past with regression. I also have a strong belief in reincarnation. I believe we come back to earth over and over again to learn and experience for our soul.

Beliefs are a very strong feeling that we all have in many different subjects. The most important thing to remember is to believe in what is true to your heart and soul, stay happy and let go of guilt for going with what you feel and as far as those who may judge you for it, in one ear and out the other. Don't let it hit your ego because that will bring back doubt. Make your heart stronger than your ego. I tell people who I am and what I do and I am proud of who I am and if they don't like it, that's fine because I respect their opinions and beliefs, and I expect the same in return.

Don't ever confuse belief with judgment. Many of us are quick to judge someone and we say "I believe they . . .". Unless you know everything and every thought of that person, you are judging them. Remember belief is truth. Would you want to be judged about what's going on in your life . . . I don't think so.

Affirmations: I know my beliefs through my Heart.

My beliefs are my truths.

I am confident in my beliefs and myself.

B—BOUNDARIES

Boundaries are a way of putting up a wall (so to say) to hold someone or something back, so as not to infringe on your space or time. How many of you right now are reading this and thinking, I don't do that. I don't let anyone over power me and take up all my time. Now think about that. How many times have you let someone spill all his or her drama on you? You may be thinking that you are being nice and lending an ear for them to vent, but how often does this happen? If it is always then you need to put up some boundaries. How many of you have and continue to always help someone out of a jam? Maybe they just need a few dollars (again), a ride somewhere, always asking you for help, and taking you away from what you need to do. Then it is time to learn to set some boundaries.

In most cases you are doing so much for everyone else and ignoring what you need done. Have you ever noticed that the favor is not returned? This makes you unbalanced. All giving and no receiving. One way of putting up boundaries is learning a simple word . . . NO. The reason people don't say no is because the guilt factor comes in and they feel bad. This is because you have a heart. Not to say that those who infringe on you don't have a heart, but they spend more time working with the ego, which allows them to be more selfish and puts their needs ahead of others. Sometimes these people are so stuck in drama or grief that they don't even notice their behavior. Then of course you do have those who know what they are doing and just don't care. They feel the world owes them something.

There is nothing wrong with saying no. As children we all heard our parents say no many times. We probably didn't like it very much but later understood why they did. So why not bring that into our adulthood. When someone is constantly pouring out their drama to you, you have to stop them and say no more, please. I care for you as a person but I ask you to stop pouring your drama over me. They probably won't like it but if they are a true friend they will understand. If they don't understand then maybe it is time to let them go.

Maybe at work you have people who dump their work on you all the time. They say please help me I have so much and can't catch up. Then to your amazement they are off doing something else, socializing, or working so slowly so as not to get their work done on time. They may even lay the guilt trip on you by saying if they don't get any help and finish the boss will be really mad. Well guess what? That is not your issue. What would happen to you if you helped them and then didn't get your own work done? Your co-worker will be all set and you will get into trouble. Believe me it is fine to help others but only if they are worth helping. Those who constantly ask for help because they don't want to do it themselves, are not the one's you should be losing your time for. You need to learn to say no or not now, but when I'm done with my work I will gladly help you out. Priorities people!! You need to take care of yourself first. Remember I am writing of those who cross those boundaries, not those who ask for a minute or two of your time on occasion.

Boundaries apply to family as well. Unfortunately foe some family can be the one's who take advantage more than anyone else. I have met many people who come to see me for readings, healing and what have you and tell me how their mother, father, husband, wife, sister, brother and so on are always crossing their boundaries. Of course they then tell me they feel obligated to help especially when it's family or they are getting dragged into the family drama. I tell them that they have a choice. We always have a choice. You do not have to help anyone, whether they are family, friend or co-worker if they are taking advantage of you.

Here is an example of family drama with no boundaries. A client told me that she was tired of her sibling who was always asking for money, only $20 he would say. She explained that she didn't have much herself but felt obligated because it was a sibling. Now the sibling is a person who didn't work, or worked sometimes, never paid the bills, but would always have money to go party. She hoped that she would be paid back. Sometimes yes, sometimes no. I explained to her that she has a choice. She needed to stop, because the more she gave in the more it was expected and that her sibling would never learn. This is her sibling's path to follow not hers. Her sibling put themselves into their situation and it was their choice. So she needs to let it go and the universe will take care of it. They both have a choice on how they want to live and to change what is not working for them.

Update. My client did finally decide that enough was enough and no longer gives in to her sibling. She has learned to put herself first and take care of what she needs to. As far as her sibling goes, well I hope they learn someday too.

I think the hardest boundary to put up is with parents. I have met many people who have so much drama with their mother, father or both. It's one thing if your parent becomes ill and needs help, believe me; I was there with my sister for our father during some difficult medical issues. All lot happened from September 2005 when our mother was diagnosed with cancer and passed away in June 2006. Then our father in 2009 was diagnosed with a brain aneurysm, which led to surgery, then a mild heart attack in February 2010 which revealed a blockage in his arteries and led to a triple by-pass. Only to find out in February of 2011 that the springs that were inserted into Dad's head had moved and here we go again, another head surgery in March of 2011 to fix the spring and add another one. My sister and I were there every step of the way from traveling to Boston Mass General several times to helping him out at home. Believe me when I tell you, our Dad was so grateful to both of us and knows we will always be there for him as much as he has always been there for us.

The boundaries people need with their parents are for those who deal with those who always expect you to put their needs before your own. Then unfortunately you have some parents who expect everything from you but will never support you in your endeavors, tell you that your not doing things right and so on. When you do finally have some time for yourself, they say, "Well you had time, why didn't you help me"? Maybe you have a parent that is on a fixed income (which is only fixed because that's how they perceive it) and you work so hard to save up some money so that you can buy something or get things done and they turn around and say, "Why did you buy that? You should have given the extra money to me, you know I don't have any". Some parents can be tough.

I can say that I am lucky to have great parents (even in spirit my Mom holds boundaries) who never infringe on my time and let me live my life, but know that I am there if needed and visa versa. We all understand each other, respect each other and we hold onto a balance of giving and receiving. I am extremely grateful for that. This is something that all human beings should do. I think if everyone spent more time in positive energy, trust, respect and understanding, Life Would Be Good!

When you have a parent that does not act in this way it can be hard. On one hand you do love them because they are your Mom and or Dad, on the other hand you may dislike them very much for what they can put you trough. This is where you need to set some boundaries. Like I mentioned previously, you have to tell them (in a loving way) that you can't do what they want you to do until you have the time because you do have your own responsibilities to tend to and those have to be first. Also if money is an issue, just explain that you cannot help at this time and you need to pay and take care of your own responsibilities. This applies to those who take advantage.

So how do you do this? I tell my clients that first you have to put your foot down and say to yourself that you are not going to be treated like this anymore, then you need to be strong and tell them how you feel and then follow through with your decision. So now you will either have a parent that truly understands or they will be very upset. If you have one of those parents who do get upset because you spoke your mind, stop for a moment and think why do they act this way? Maybe there is a reason. They may have been brought up this way and that's all they know, they could be holding onto anger, they could be jealous because their children have more than they ever did or any other reason. Whatever the reason, remember their issue is not your issue. We are all here to learn a lesson and follow our own path. So if they are not learning and have fallen off their path, which is for them to figure out and fix. You have to let it go. All you can do is send them love and light and pray that they find their way.

Always look at everyone and everything with love. The more you send them love the better. Think of it like this. Lets you have a grandparent who is getting very forgetful due to age or illness. They constantly repeat themselves and maybe becoming unsafe to home alone. Do you get mad and irritated with them or do you stop and think to yourself that it's because of age or illness? You understand that they may not know what they are doing and you just hold compassion for them. Now do that with everyone else. When you have someone who irritates you, think to yourself that maybe they do this because _____. Just hold love and light for them and be compassionate. Another reason could be that God has put these people in your path to teach you something. Think of someone that irritates you, what is it they do that irritates you and now look at yourself and see how that applies to your life. Remember putting up boundaries doesn't mean push people out of your life, but set limits. Love and Let Go!

B—BREATHWORK

Breathwork is an amazing spiritual exercise that brings release and clarity. I hold Breathwork sessions at my center and it is the most amazing way of letting go of what is buried deep within us that no longer serves us.

I remember my first Breathwork session that I tried at a spiritual retreat I had gone to. It was very powerful, but at first questioned what can just breathing do? Well I released so much that day and finally had peace with a situation I had gone through during my younger years and thought I was over it, but truly I wasn't. I felt so much better after it was over. I had no idea that breathing would do so much for me. So this is when I decided that this was something I needed to bring to my center so my clients could benefit just like I did. This is a way for me to help people heal.

How does Breathwork work? First everyone lies on the floor with mats, blankets and pillows to be comfortable. I pass out eye masks to everyone. This helps to keep out distractions and keeps things dark so you can see with your third eye vision clearer. Music is played loud. It can be instrumental, Songs with words, meditation music, vibrational music or whatever spirit guides me to use. The music is played loud because it helps with the process of healing as well as drowns out the sounds of others as they experience emotions during breathwork.

Next we start everyone doing the breathing. This is done with circular breathing. Breathing in deeply through the mouth, like you are sucking through a straw and then releasing your breath through the mouth hard. You do not breath through the nose at all it is all mouth breathing. As you begin to do this with in minutes you begin to release issues. Now I truly believe that our soul knows what needs to be released first, so it can be something from your distant past, present or anything in between. It is possible to release more than one issue during your breathwork session.

As your issue(s) start to come to the forefront you may start crying, and this is a good thing. This means you are letting go of what no longer serves you. People have been known to laugh, chant, sing, moan and/or cry or whatever other way the body wishes to express itself. As the issue(s) start to release and you are expressing emotion, especially crying, you need to continue the breathing. You need to breathe through it, breathe through the emotional pain. I tell the women that it is like labor, when the pain hits . . . breathe. Some people do experience pain or discomfort and this is because emotions can come out as pain in the body. Same here, breathe through it. This is not something that happens very often, usually it is just a discomfort but if it does then just breathe through it until it subsides.

Other experiences people have during Breathwork. Many people have visions and it is usually what you are releasing that is shown to you. This is what happened to me. I saw the person that I had issues with when they were here on earth. I finally had my chance to express my feelings since I hadn't done it when they were here. During this time I was able to resolve everything. Most people can see during Breathwork, but if you don't, not to worry. You may also feel, sense, know or hear what needs to be released and who is involved. Breathwork can be intense for some people, usually the first time. It gets easier every time you do it. It all depends on what you need to release and let go of. Now for those who have let go of a lot may have great visions during Breathwork. They can also have a sense of peacefulness, harmony and love. Messages are also received during Breathwork. They can come from your Angels, Guides or loved ones who have passed on.

Breathwork sessions can last from 2 hours to 4 or 6 hours. I do only 2-hour sessions at my center. When I tell my clients this they ask how anyone could breathe like that for so long. Believe me I said the same thing the first time I did it. I was shocked to look at the clock and see that 2 and a half hours had passed since the start. It felt like only 30 minutes to an hour had gone by. So much happens during Breathwork that there is no concept of time.

During Breathwork you may experience tingling in your hands and feet. This is normal. It is because your taking in so much oxygen at once that the body is not used to it and this tingling can happen. For those with asthma there is nothing to worry about. Everyone I know that has asthma and has done Breathwork, has never had a problem. If anything it is good exercise for your lungs.

If for any reason you cannot lay on the floor Breathwork can be done sitting in a chair. It does work just as well. Just be sure that you are comfortable and have a blanket handy. Some people do get cold when they do Breathwork. Another point here is that I do not recommend doing Breathwork alone, because it can be very emotional and when we get emotional, we forget to keep breathing. This is why it is good to do it at a group session. We coach you along the way and keep you breathing in that circular technique. Also as a Reiki Master, I can help those who are experiencing pain or discomfort with healing energy being applied as they continue to breathe.

I truly believe that Breathwork is the fastest way to release old issues quickly. It still takes work to release what no longer serves us, but Breathwork sure does bring it to the forefront. The more you do it the more you releases and the better you will feel. You will get to the point that once you have released as much as you need to, your Breathwork sessions will be more uplifting and peaceful.

What people have told me they have experienced after breathwork:

* Released issue that they had put behind locked doors, because it was to painful.
* Having visions of something they couldn't have experienced here.
* Had a vision of a loved one from the other side and spent time with them.
* Released things that they had forgotten had even happened.
* Felt someone touching them during the session (usually an Angel, guide or loved one).
* Let go of bad feelings about themselves.
* Felt so good after the session, like a weight had been lifted, more clarity.
* Received messages and guidance.

So as you can see Breathwork is very beautiful. The more you release, the better you will feel. As I have written throughout this book, you need to let things go in order to be able to move forward. I truly advise that you try Breathwork and do it more than once. The more you do the better you will feel. It is the perfect way of letting go.

C—CHAKRAS

Chakras (pronounced Sha Kra) are energy centers within the body. We have thousands of charkas throughout the body. As a healer I work mainly with the 7 main charkas and as Reiki Master I work with hand charkas that have been opened so that I can pass healing energy onto others. Highly intuitive people who can hear spirit have their ear charkas open. We all have feet charkas, which we should all use. The charkas in the feet are what keep us grounded.

Every chakra has it's own color, energy and each corresponds with different parts of the body. For example if you are having stomach issues, your solar plexus is off. The energy may be low and the color is dull in that chakra. When I do healings on clients, I can see the charkas, the color and if the chakra is in good shape or not. Not all oarctitioners can see the charkas. Some can see just the color, some sense what the charkas are like or they may just know through their intuitive guidance how the charkas are.

I realized one day back in 2006 that I could see the charkas. It was during a Reiki session with a client, when I heard, just ask to see them and they will show you. So I asked in my mind, show me this persons charkas. Sure enough I saw the images of 7 spinning wheels of all different colors from the top of their head to the base of their spine.

The word chakra means, spinning wheel in Sanskrit. So in a balanced and healthy body all 7 chakras will be colorful and spinning in the proper direction. Each chakra spins in a certain direction and speed. The lower charkas spin slowly and as you move up towards the crown the faster they spin. The first 3 lower charkas spin in a counter clockwise direction, the 4th, 5th and 6th chakra spin in a clockwise direction and the crown chakra (7th) spins in a counter clockwise direction.

Not only physical issues can affect your charkas, but emotional or mental issues can have an effect as well. Have you ever felt off, not yourself, out of sorts and so on? This means that there is some sort of emotional/mental imbalance and it is showing up in your charkas. More than likely it is your solar plexus and/or sacral chakra that will be off. These are your energy and emotion centers. As I said earlier every chakra corresponds with a part of the body, an emotion and mental issues, so here is a list of the 7 chakras, their colors, where in the body they are and the physical and emotional/mental issues that are connected to them.

#7—Crown chakra (white or purple)—
    Top of the head
#6—Third Eye chakra (Indigo)—
    Center of forehead between the eye brows
#5—Throat chakra(Blue)—
    Throat
#4—Heart chakra—(Green)—
    Center of the chest
#3—Solar Plexus (yellow)—
    Just above the naval
#2—Sacral chakra (Orange)—
    Just below the naval
#1—Root chakra (Red)—
    Base of the spine

Physical Connections:

Crown: Pineal gland, hair, top of head, central nervous system

Third eye: Pituitary gland, hypothalamus, eyes, autonomic nervous system

Throat: Thyroid, parathyroid, neck, ears, respiratory system, colds, sinus, allergies

Heart: Thymus, heart, breathing, lungs, blood pressure, lymph, immune system

Solar Plexus: Pancreas, stomach, liver, small intestine, blood sugar, digestion

Sacral: Ovaries, urinary tract, uterus, kidneys, adrenal glands, spleen

Root: Sex/Reproduction system, rectum, tailbone, legs and feet

Emotional/Mental Connections:

Crown: Compassion, at oneness, seeing self in others, allowing ness, harmonious

Peaceful, non-attached, loving, non-reactive, spirit love

Third Eye: Overview, visualizing, clairvoyance, choice of good for all,

Psychic/subtle awareness of self, others, addictions healed, service

Throat: Open clear communicating feelings, thoughts, creativity, speaking up

Releasing, breathing life force, healing

Heart: Harmony, trust, lovingness, gentle with others, able to give and receive,

Flexible, open to new people, ideas, growth, coping with loss, balance

Solar Plexus: Mental energy, will power/control over self VS. others, beliefs

Details, constructive VS. self critical thoughts, perfection

Sacral: Feeling, emotional needs, boundaries, trust, warmth, intimacy, attach/let

Go, addiction, pleasure, joy, begin/end

Root: Body and money needs, safety, sexuality, actions, grounded ness, physical energy.

This is a partial list of the physical, emotional and mental connections with the charkas. There is so much more. You have the power to figure out what is bothering you and which chakra is affected. All you need to do is sit quietly and listen to your body. Feel or sense what is out if sync. Our bodies are very good at telling us that there is something wrong, as long as we listen. We tend to ignore these feelings and signs. Then we just live with the feeling thinking that it is normal. Think of a time when you felt completely balanced, everything was good, you were happy and so on. How did your body feel? Does it feel like that now? If it does, then you are balanced. If not then pay attention to what your body is telling you. Look at your life and see what is not working. Are things off at home, work, family or friends? Maybe you're just overall unbalanced and it seems like everything in your life is wrong and falling apart. Is your health not good?

Here is a meditation that you can use to clear and heal your charkas. If you are not visual, don't worry, use all your senses, and feel see, hear, sense and know. Most important is the intention. Intention is everything. First find yourself a quiet place to meditate. Now close your eyes and take 3 deep breaths, in through the nose and exhale out through the mouth (this helps you to relax faster). Continue with meditation:

Visualize a ball of red light at your feet. Breathe in this red light right into your root chakra and feel as it cleans, recharges and balances your chakra.

Visualize a ball of orange light at your feet. Breathe in this orange light right into your sacral chakra and feel as it cleans, recharges and balances your chakra.

Visualize a ball of yellow light at your feet. Breathe in this yellow light right into your solar plexus chakra and feel as it cleans, recharges and balances your chakra.

Visualize a ball of green light at your feet. Breathe in this green light right into your heart chakra and feel as it cleans, recharges and balances your chakra.

Visualize a ball of pink light at your feet. Breathe in this pink light right into your heart chakra and feel as it merges with the green and brings love into your heart.

Visualize a ball of blue light at your feet. Breathe in this blue light right into your throat chakra and feel as it cleans, recharges and balances your chakra.

Visualize a ball of indigo light at your feet. Breathe in this indigo light right into your third eye chakra and feel as it cleans, recharges and balances your chakra.

Visualize a ball of violet light at your feet. Breathe in this violet light right into your crown chakra and feel as it cleans, recharges and balances your chakra.

Now visualize a beam of gold light coming down from above. See this light completely surround you from head to toe, sealing in all the color and energy. Hold this visual for as long as you can. Now the gold light retreats back up to the heavens, leaving you filled with its light and energy. Take a few moments to feel the energy from yor head to the feet. Notice how much better you feel. When you are ready, take a deep breath and open your eyes. This is a simple meditation to help you to pay attention to how you feel and how you can feel even better when you are in balance.

Affirmation: My body is in perfect balance, mentally, emotionally, physically and spiritually.

C—CRYSTALS

Crystals have been used for thousands of years in healing practices. Each one has it's own energy and vibration. With a little practice you too can feel its energy vibrating in your hand. Some crystals are stronger than others. There are hundreds of different crystals and they each have a purpose. Healers, readers, and every other spiritual practice that I can think of use Crystals. You don't have to be one of these to use them. I sell crystals at my center. I have many clients that come in and buy them for many different purposes. Crystals are used for many different reasons like love, abundance, protection, prosperity, illness, meditation, and so much more.

I use crystals for healings. I might use them during a Reiki session if I am guided to do so. I use them for specifically doing crystal healings. This is when I have the client lay down and place crystals on their body. I use the crystals that correspond with the chakras. Then I clear out the chakras and send energy through the crystals to the body. Meditations are a time when I may put crystals out. When we do a chakra meditation I will set up a crystal grid on the floor in the center of the circle.

How does someone pick a crystal for himself or herself? First you need to know what it is that you want to do or heal. Then figure out which crystal you need that corresponds with the issue at hand. When you go to buy one make sure that you connect with the crystal. Don't just grab one and run out of the store. You want to connect with it. Hold the crystal in your hand. Does it feel good? Does it have good energy? Once you decide on a crystal then your ready to take it or them home.

Cleansing your crystals: You want to clean your crystals before you use them, because they have been touched by many other people at the store you got them from. Not including the fact they were handled in the company that distributes them. So there can be a lot of different energy in your crystal(s). There is many different ways to clean your crystals. Use which ever method you prefer.

- A simple method to clean crystals is to use the healing abilities of water and the sun. Let cold water pour over the crystal(s) and then let them dry in the sun for 30 minutes. After just polish with a clean cloth.

- For new stones and crystals it is recommended to submerge them in salt for at least 3 hours (1 cup sea salt to 2 cups cold water) rinse and let dry in the sun.

- Recharge the crystal with Reiki energy by holding it in your hand and let the energy flow into it (if you are a Reiki practitioner) Reiki II & III can use the symbols to recharge and cleanse crystals.

- Crystals that have been misused or depleted of the energy can be submerged in dry sea salt for 3 days, rinse in cool water and let dry in the sun.

- Crystals can also be used to cleanse and purify other crystals, healing stone and jewelry.

Here is a list of different crystals and their metaphysical purposes.

Agate
Balances ying-yang energy, stabilizes the aura. Facilitates discernment. Imparts strength and courage. Opens one to innate creative talents. (There are many forms of agate, each with specific properties.)

Amber
Purifies body, mind, and spirit. Balances electromagnetics of the body and allows even flow of energies. Provides a positive, soothing energy. Spiritualizes the intellect.

Amethyst
Sedative energy. Facilitates spirituality and contentment. Stone of stability, strength, and peace. Excellent for meditation. Enhances psychic ability.

Aventurine
Independence, leadership, creativity. Balances male/female energies. Aligns mental, physical, emotional, and auric bodies.

Aquamarine
Courage, intellect, protection. Assists spiritual awareness, actualization.

Azurite
Awakens psychic ability, insight, intuition. Third eye. Excellent for clearing the mind in meditation.

Apache Tears
Assists in the grieving process, and allows forgiveness. Breaks down the barriers that hold one back. Also good for the analytical mind.

Amazonite
Balancing energy, harmony, universal love.

Calcite
Energy amplifier, teacher. Optical Calcite is excellent for clearing and cleansing.

Celestite
Excellent stone for dream recall and astral travel. Hope and harmony. Communication.

Chrysocolla
Strength, balance. Promotes harmony and attunement to the earth. Purifies one's environment.

Chrysoprase
Balances yin-yang energy. Acceptance of self and others.

Citrine
Positive energy—stone needs no cleansing. Dissipates negative energy. Warmth, joy, optimism.

Copal
Excellent for strengthening the abilities of the mind, and altered states of consciousness. Amplifies one's energy field.

Diamond
Purity, perfection, abundance, inspiration.

Emerald
Loyalty, sensitivity, harmony, tranquility. Assists in memory retention and mental clarity.

Fluorite
Stability, order, discernment, concentration. Helps one to understand and maintain ideals and the perfection of the universe.

Garnet
Commitment, devotion, love, stability and order. Even flow of energy.

Gold
Spirituality, understanding, attunement to nature. Attracts positive energy. Excellent healer.

Hematite
Excellent for the mind. Grounding.

Herkimer Diamond
Awareness, attunement, clairvoyance, telepathy. Good for information retention.

Jade
Harmony, peace, fidelity, confidence. A wonderful dream stone.

Jasper
Protection, awareness, insight. Grounding.

Kunzite
Communication, love, peace. Protects and dissolves negativity. Excellent for meditation.

Kyanite
Never needs cleaning or clearing, aligns all chakras. Tranquility, communication, psychic awareness. Excellent for meditation and dream recall.

Labradorite
Represents the light of the universe, extra-terrestrial energy. Intuition, subconscious. Illumination.

Lapis Lazuli
Knowledge, wisdom, perfection, protection, creative expression.

Lepidolite
Honesty, stability, hope, acceptance. Assists in change and transition. Facilitates astral travel.

Malachite
Transformation, spiritual development. Clears the way to attain goals. Fidelity, loyalty, reasoning ability.

Moldavite
Clarity, eternity. Extra-terrestrial, interdimensional access.

Moonstone
Lunar, female energy. Emotional, intuitive. Rhythms, cycles, destiny.

Obsidian
Dispels negativity. Grounding, healing, protective. Helps one to clearly see one's flaws and the changes that are necessary.

Onyx
Centering, self-control, intuitive guidance. Assists in the grieving process.

Opal
Creativity, inspiration, imagination.

Peridot
Healing, protective. Allows one to understand changes in one's life, regulates life cycles.

Petrified Wood
Grounding, provides strength. Stone of transformation.

Pyrite
Shields from negative energy, good stone of protection. Enhances intellect and memory. Symbol of the sun.

Quartz Crystal (clear)
Universal crystal, clarity of consciousness . . . . see the quartz crystal page for complete info.

Rhodochrosite
Love energy. Excellent stone for balance in all areas.

Ruby
Loving, nurturing, spirituality, wealth, protection.

Rutilated Quartz
Intensifies energy of the crystal. Stimulates brain. Inspiration, clairvoyance.

Sapphire
Joy, peace, beauty, prosperity.

Selenite (Gypsum)
Clarity of consciousness, awareness, insight, good judgement. Aids in accessing past/future lives.

Silver
Mirror to the soul. Eloquence. Connects physical and astral bodies. In jewelry, it provides a balanced setting that retains the qualities of the stone it holds. Lunar energy. Cleansing, balancing.

Smoky Quartz
Dissolves negativity, grounding, balancing. Excellent for meditation.

Sodalite
Logic, efficiency, truthfulness. Enhances group communication.

Sugilite
Spiritual love, perfection, inspiration, confidence. Alleviates negative/destructive emotions.

<u>Tigereye</u>
Earthy, grounding. Represents sun and earth. Optimism, insight, personal power.
<u>Topaz</u>
Success, true love, individuality, creativity, joy.
<u>Tourmaline</u>
Inspiration, understanding, self-confidence, balancing. Electrical.
<u>Tourmalinated Quartz</u>
Strength, balancing. Combines attributes of tourmaline and quartz.
<u>Turquoise</u>
Spiritual attunement, strength, grounding. Protective—excellent for astral travel.
<u>Zircon</u>
Virtue, unification, continuity, purity.

List of crystals and their healing properties.

Abundance. . . . . Citrine
Addictions/Alcoholism . . . . Amethyst
Allergies. . . . . .Chrysocolla, Carnelian
Anger . . . . Carnelian, Howlite
Arthritis. . . . . Malachite, Copper
Blood Pressure. . . . . .Bloodstone
Circulation System . . . . Hematite
Bones . . . . Calcite
Calming. . . . . Lepidolite
Courage . . . . .Aquamarine
Creativity. . . . . .Azurite
Depression. . . . . .Lapis Lazuli
Detoxification . . . . Covellite
Fidelity. . . . . Jade
Grief. . . . . Obsidian, Apache Tears
Harmony . . . . Sodalite
Headache. . . . . .Sugalite, Ruby
Immune System. . . . . .Lapis Lazuli
Digestive System . . . . Citrine
Leg Cramps . . . . .Bloodstone
Mental Clarity. . . . . Quartz Crystal

Fertility . . . . Chrysoprase
Heart . . . . Copal, Chrysoprase
Fever. . . . . Hematite
Sleep. . . . . Jade, Lepidolite
Stress . . . . Lepidolite
Eyes . . . . Celestite, Labradorite
Purify Body/Mind/Spirit . . . . Amber

Crystals and the chakra system

Below is a basic listing of stones and their corresponding chakra to get you started.

Root Chakra. . . . . .Ruby
Sacral Chakra . . . . Orange Calcite
Solar Plexus. . . . . Citrine
Heart . . . . Rose Quartz
Throat. . . . . Lapis Luzuli
Third Eye . . . . Amethyst
Crown Chakra . . . . .Clear Quartz

There are hundreds of crystals out there and I think these lists will help get you started. Be sure to carry your crystal around with you either on your person or in your handbag. Ladies you cam also put your crystal in your bra, we call that boob stones. Be sure to connect with your crystal by cleaning it first then holding it in your hand and putting in the intention of what it is meant to do and what you want it to do.

D—DIVINE GUIDANCE

Divine guidance is a message that you receive from God, the Angels, ascended masters/teachers, guides or anyone else from the highest vibration of light. These messages can come in many different forms. You can receive it yourself through your own intuition, from a card reader or an intuitive.

When you receive the message yourself, you may get it through hearing a voice or thought in your head, seeing something that pertains to what you have asked for help with, feeling (like a gut feeling), or just a knowing. The divine also like to leave items in front of us to find such as, coins, feathers and repetitive numbers. There are so many ways of receiving guidance; we just have to open ourselves up to it so we can get them. Many call these signs coincidence. There is no such thing. Everything happens for a reason. Sometimes we are just so full of anger, worry, stress and so on, that we miss the signs and messages. We don't see what is right in front of us.

How many times did you get a gut feeling or a thought and went against it? Many times I'm sure. The problem is many people don't trust what they are feeling. They think they are crazy, they made it up or that is was just your imagination. If everyone would learn to just go with it, they would see how it does work. Your gut is never wrong. Divine guidance can help us with decisions, following our path, opening up more to spirit, helping us to change, or even protect us when something is about to happen.

Here is a time when I went against what I was hearing in my head. I was heading to my center after volunteering at the hospital, when I decided to go a different way. From this direction I could have gone two ways. I could have taken the highway or gone the back roads. Well as I approached that area, I heard "take the highway". Well at first I was like "what"? Then I heard it again. Now I need to change lanes and it was not going to happen. There were cars around me. So I proceeded to take the back roads. I could have made a u turn further up the road, but I said, "Oh well" and just kept going. This is when I should have known that this was not going to be good. About a mile and a half from my center I was coming up on a store on my right and looking ahead I saw a driver wanting to turn into the store from the oncoming traffic side. Well this is what the angels were warning me about. Just as I was in front of the store the older gentleman on the other side decided he wanted the parking spot right in front and without looking he crossed over right in front of me. Well of course I hit him and hard. Luckily neither one of us got hurt. My car was banged up but his was not drivable. If I had really listened, I could have avoided this . . . lesson learned! So listen and pay attention, your guidance is never wrong.

Another example of divine guidance is when my sister and I were looking for a place to open our healing center. Every time I was driving I would look for a place for rent. There is a place here where we live that I would drive by many times in a week, but even though there was assign that said for rent, I could never see the empty space. I remember saying to the angels, "please help me to find the perfect place for me and Dora where we could start our healing center". One day coming up on this place while driving home it was like someone took my steering wheel and made me turn into the lot. So I said Ok and went into the office that was there and inquired about the space for rent. Well to my surprise she informed me that there is a space available and tells me to follow her. She then takes me down a back stairway to a lower level. Well when we walked in I couldn't believe it. It was everything I asked for. There were two treatment rooms, a waiting area and a front desk. We even had our own private entrance in the back with a parking lot.

I called my sister so she could see it and as soon as she saw it, we took it! All we had to do was paint and move our stuff in. We opened two weeks after that day on March 1, 2006 and Sisters of Solace was born. A big Thank You to Debbie for renting to us and giving us the chance to bring love, light and healing to all who seek it.

I use divine guidance as a daily practice. I call upon the angels everyday to guide me in decision-making, getting what I need and what I want. Right down to the smallest things such as a parking space close to the door at the mall. The angels always guide me and give me messages. If for some reason I don't get it the first time they do repeat the messages again and again until I do. Remember I'm no better than anyone else, I still have an ego that likes to get in the way and I do my best just like all of you to keep my ego at bay. The biggest thing about your ego is recognizing when it's getting in the way. If you can get to that part, you are doing good! Keep up the good work.

Ever notice how you hear or see something three times? Maybe your thinking about going back to school and someone says something about you should. Then you see a commercial on TV for the school that is offering what you need. Then third, your reading the newspaper and there is another ad for the same school. Well guess what, here's your sign. The divine has brought you three signs that pertains to what you need answers for. Follow it!

Another way divine guidance comes through is by ideas that just pop into your head. Did you ever feel like there is something your supposed to be doing but don't know what it is? Well the divine is down loading (as I call it) information into your sub conscious. They are getting you ready for what is coming up for you. Be patient and when the time is right it will be revealed to you. They will send you the signs, messages and open things up for you so that it can happen. This is when the ideas pop into your head. Also have ever had a conversation with yourself in your head? Well your not talking to yourself, you are talking with the divine. People tell me all the time that it can't be because it is their own voice. Well of course it is, it's your body. How else could you ask a question and answer it? Listen when this happens, you can get a lot from it.

This book is an example of divine guidance. About a year and half before I starting writing this book, a friend of mine gave me a message from my mother (who is passed). She wanted to know where the book was. I thought to myself, what is she talking about? My friend explained that my mother told her that I should be writing the book and wanted to know what I was waiting for? Well I was dumb founded. Me write a book? I don't know anything about writing a book or even where to begin. What am I supposed to write about? My friend gave me an idea about what it should be called and I did use that. Thank You Lorianne for the guidance and message from my mother! Without you I don't know how long it would have taken me to get those messages.

Well in February of 2011 I started getting signs about writing the book. The signs came from everywhere. They came fast and furious. Everyone I talked to mentioned about me writing a book, I saw ads for "Learn how to write your own book" and so much more. So I told my divine beings, "ok, ok I get it I will write a book. So I got started. Once I was open to the fact of writing this book, I asked my angels to guide me as what to write and where to begin. Well that's all it took. The ideas and words were flying into my head so fast I had trouble keeping up. Here is the wonderful result of all that guidance, a book that I hope you enjoy and learn from.

Please be patient. Sometimes we have to wait for the right time to do what we are guided to do. Everything happens when it is supposed to and how it is supposed to. Good comes to those who wait!

Earlier I wrote about ways of receiving guidance and here are the terms used to define the different ways to get guidance.

* Clairvoyance—the ability to psychically see
* Clairaudience—the ability to hear spirit
* Clairsentience—the ability to feel spirit
* Claircognizance—the ability to have clear thinking

Clairvoyance: to see clearly through means of your physical vision or spiritual vision (third eye/minds eye). Example; dreams, visions, signs, coins, feathers, butterflies, birds, rainbows, TV ads, repetitive numbers and the such.

Clairaudience: to clearly hear through your physical ears or inner hearing (that voice in your head). Example; Having that conversation with yourself in your head, hearing outside your head, hear your name called when no one is there, hearing angelic or other music, high pitched buzzing in one ear, hearing a conversation someone else is having and it pertains to what you are seeking help with, certain song on the radio comes on that sounds like it was written just for you or may remind you of a loved one that has passed and this is their way of saying hello.

Clairsentience: To have clear feelings. Such as emotions of joy, sadness or other emotions that don't belong to you, but you are picking up on from others. Sensing that spirit is in the room with you, feeling warmth around you when there is no heat source, feeling cold spots when there is no draft. Smells can also be a feeling. Think of how you feel when you smell certain scents. They may remind you of a loved one that has passed or maybe they just bring you a total sense of happiness or peace.

Claircognizance: To have clear thinking. Example; to know something with out knowing where it came from. Ability to put together or fix things without prior knowledge of how to do it or instructions. Having a Aha moment, saying just the right thing to someone who needs an encouraging word (without knowing where it came from). Also getting ideas in a way, like someone placed it in your head and you have one of those I knew that was going to happen moments.

We all have this intuition. One "Clair" may be stronger than another. Pay attention to which "Clair" is strongest for you. Do you find that you are very visual? Do you listen attentively? Find yourself saying "I felt that was right" or "I knew that"? So focus on which one you are and use that to connect to the divine and be open to the other ways as well. The other "Clairs" can develop more too, the more you practice.

Here is a simple meditation that you can use to connect to the divine. First find a quiet and comfortable place where you will not be disturbed. Take 2-3 deep breaths to relax yourself. Breathe in through the nose and breathe out through your mouth (this helps you to relax faster). Then Begin . . . .

Connecting With The Divine

Dear Angels, please help me to be open to your guidance and the guidance from all those of the highest vibration of light. I ask that you keep me protected and surrounded by love and the white light. Now visualize yourself in a beautiful garden. See the flowers, trees, shrubs, colors, smell the scents. Pay attention to anything in your garden. Hear the sounds of the birds singing. There are two beautiful chairs in the center of your garden. Sit in one and ask your angel, guide or anyone from the divine to join you. When they have, ask them questions; who they are, what their name is, if they have a message for you or you can ask a question and then wait for a response. Spend a few minutes with them. When you feel that you are done speaking with them, show your gratitude and slowly start to bring your awareness back and take a deep breath and open your eyes.

Now take some time to journal your experience. Write down everything you saw, head, felt and sensed. Use this meditation as often as you want. Use it, practice with it and get those "Clairs" open. The more you practice the more you will open up and the easier it gets.

Remember anytime you need direction, guidance or answers; always call upon the divine for help. They are more than willing to help when you ask.

Affirmation: I AM connected to the divine.

I AM open to receiving Messages.

I easily receive messages.

D—DRAMA

Drama is the unnecessary evil that people create or push onto others and can be like a plague that can spread from one person to another. Warning, warning, warning!!!! Stay away from the drama and don't be the one who creates the drama. Drama will keep you so far away from the light and that is NOT where you want to be.

All drama is, is living through the EGO! It can be called gossip, judgment and so many other names. This book is intended to show you how to live in harmony with love and light. I didn't want any negativity brought into it, but I feel you need to know about the negativity because it is out there and it is very easy to get caught up in it. You want o learn to let it go or be protected from it so you don't absorb it. You will learn how to live a life of hope, harmony and happiness.

Drama is when someone has issues in their life that they continue to dwell on instead of looking for ways to improve it. Then they proceed to drag everyone they know into it. Of course we have the choice of whether or not to indulge in it. If you do decide to indulge in someone else's drama, you are making their issues your own. For example: Lets say "Sue" gets in a argument with "Jane". Now you step in and argue with Jane because Sue is your friend. Now we have a three-way fight going. STOP! First thing is that what ever happened between Jane and Sue had nothing to do with you. This is where you need to stand back and let them work things out. Your still sues friend and you can be there for her in other ways. Do not involve yourself in the drama. Stay away from issues that are not yours. You can always send love and prayers to the people involved or the situation. You may not know the whole story either between the two people involved. There could be underlying issues that brought up the argument. Unless you wear someone else's shoes, you don't know everything.

I have had my run ins with drama. Years ago I did join in the "drama Club". I was one of those people who would judge and talk gossip until I found my spiritual path. Through my journey I have learned to let things go. I no longer involve myself in others issues. I will be there to listen and offer help, but I do not hold it as my own. I came to realize that people have issues going on at times and when they are mean or rude, I think right away that maybe that person has something going on and that's why they act the way they do. I just send them love and light. As an energy healer I do hear many stories of people who are going through a lot, but want to make positive changes. I do everything I can to help and then I have to let it go. Believe me I do feel compassion for those who come to me and my center. I do want to help but if I took in everyone's issues, I would be useless. I would probably end up in such negativity, that I would be living in my ego. I am here to teach and help people to learn to let go, heal and see things in a more positive light.

You maybe saying "I have this person who is always dumping their stuff on me, what do I do to get them to stop"? To me those people are like leeches. They grab on and don't let go. Then expect you to have all the answers and change things for you. You know it is great to have someone to talk to and get advise but then you do help and they refuse to change because they like the drama better, know that there is only so much you can do. There comes a time when you have to say Enough! That's when you just need to tell this person, No more! You may even have to let this person go as a friend. We do hate letting go of so-called friends, because we feel guilty. But can you really afford to stay with someone who is constantly bringing you down, drains your energy and refuses to change?

If you are in a situation where you can't get away from this person or situation because it is a family member, then you need to learn to let it go and not indulge yourself in their issues. I tell people, it's like when your kids are small and they are playing and getting loud (we know how loud that can be) we somehow can just tune it out. It goes in one ear and out the other. I then ask them if you could do that then, then why is it we don't carry that over into our personal lives, block people out. Let their drama go in one ear and out the other.

Remember that the light is brighter and stronger than the dark. You can and will prevail over the negativity. It is your choice. Where would you rather be? How do you want to feel? How do you want to live? I choose love, light, happiness, joy and uplifting positive energy!

There are ways to protect yourself from the drama. Ask the angels to protect you. Ask that they surround you with the white light so that the negativity cannot penetrate through. Ask God and the angels to help you manifest only people of the highest and best for you. When you do have to be in the company of negative people try this. Visualize in your mind that baby pink roses are showering down all over thee people who are negative. Believe me this works so well. I use it and tell my clients to do it as well. This person that you are sending roses to will either get up and leave the room or shut their mouth. I gets calls all the time from people who tell me that tried it and wow how it worked so well! Remember sending pink roses will do the trick, because it represents love and light and what does negativity not like . . . . the light!

We all have to deal with drama throughout our lives whether it is with home, family, friends, co-workers and so on but how you choose to deal with it is up to you. Please live in the positive and the light. We are tested many times in life, so do your best to pass the test. It's a lifelong practice to be positive and it will get easier the more you do it. Just like anything else that we have to learn in life. We start with baby steps. You have to learn to crawl before you can walk. So please have patience with yourself and don't give up. We are all a work in progress.

Affirmations: I choose to live in harmony.
I let go of what no longer serves me.
I now have peace in my life.

E—EAR CANDLING

Ear Candling is a centuries old practice that was also done by the Egyptians, India, Chinese, American Indians and many more cultures. Today it is still practiced by those cultures and here in the US holistic healers like myself practice it. Ear Candling is a non invasive and safe way to gently remove excess wax, virus, bacteria, and it helps with sinus, allergies, swimmers ear, hearing loss, ringing in the ears, dizziness, vertigo, colds, ear infections and more. It can be done on children (as long as they can sit still) and adults. The only time you cannot have candling done is if you have tubes in your ears or if you have a perforated eardrum.

The process of doing an ear candling session is very relaxing for the client. The client lies on a massage table. Meditation music is played in the background. The cones or candles that I use are made of 100% cotton or muslin cloth dipped in a paraffin wax. They are 12 inches long and hollow. There is a small end, which is placed in the client's ear, and the large end is lit with a match. The smoke from the candle comes out the small end and when placed in the ear the smoke reverses and pulls up the candle and draws out the wax or impurities. While this is happening, I massage the face, mostly around the sinus, nasal area and the neck (lymph area). Massaging helps to break up any congestion and to push any fluid towards the ear so it can be drawn up the candle. When the candle is about 3 inches left on it, I remove it from the ear, put out the flame and then cut it open so you can see what was pulled out. I know it doesn't sound good, but everyone is always fascinated with what comes out. In fact I have even had people ask to take the candles home so they can show everyone. To each his own.

The whole session takes about 45 minutes. It requires 2 candles in each ear. For anyone with heavy-duty earwax or over packed wax may have to come back in 4-5 days to have it done again. You can't do too much candling in a short period of time; it could dry out the ears too much.

My clients love having it done. They tell me that they have better hearing, cleaner ears and it was so relaxing between the face massage and the sound of the candle burning. It sounds like a crackling fireplace.

Ear candling has so many benefits. In fact many cultures that do ear candling believe that the candling cleanses the soul as well. Lifting away any bad energy from the body and soul. People ask me why they have never heard of it, is it new? I explain the history of candling to them. I think what has happened is that as the world progressed and we became more and more advanced in medicine and science, we forgot about those great home remedies. Also people have thought how it is easier to just take a pill or drops for any ailment. Well the old ways are making a comeback. This is all part of holistic healing, healing naturally. Especially today with these medicines that have more side effects than I can count. Fix one thing and create 7 more with the side effects.

Other tricks to help your ears. Feel like you have wax build up, try using plain old olive oil and place a cotton ball in your ear. Do you know that if you buy earwax removal drops, they are made of oil with chemicals added? Also do you get swimmers ear? Try placing a few drops of alcohol in your ear, the alcohol dries up the water. Keep your head tilted for a few minutes and place a cotton ball in your ear. Don't buy swimmers eardrops. Read the ingredients, it is made up of 95% alcohol. Don't waste your money on something that you probably already have at home. So as you can see these old home remedies do work. Let's not let the old ways phase out. It's healthy and no side effects.

Some of you may or have checked this out on the internet or asked your Doctor about it. You will get pro's and con's. I feel there is nothing wrong with doing ear candling. Some Doctors disagree and don't believe in holistic healing at all. Some people are just too scientific and only believe in the medical ways to treat issues and that's fine too. Everyone is entitled to the own opinion.

I have had so much success with ear candling that you can't change my mind. I have been doing my own children's ears since they were five years old. Any time they told me that their ears were starting to hurt, I would candle their ears and no more ear infections. They have not had one infection since I started doing ear candling for them.

I have heard so many stories of people who go to the Doctors office for ear wax removal and leave bleeding. That is not right, nor does it sound safe to me. You see Doctors use this hook I call a crochet hook to remove the wax and end up scraping the inner ear and making it bleed. I have also heard of Doctors pushing hearing aids on people who don't need them. One woman that came to see me said her doctor told her that and she said no way and came to see me for ear candling. Well after her session she could hear just fine, it was a buildup of wax, that's it. I truly believe there is a conspiracy between doctors, drug companies and pharmaceuticals to make a lot of money, but that's only my opinion and we won't go there!

Ear Candles are available in many health food or holistic stores which the public can purchase. I do not advise anyone to do their own ears. I feel it is dangerous to try and do your own ears with a flaming candle burning over your head and you can't see it. I recommend that you have your ears done by a professional or someone you know that has done it before and knows what they are doing.

Ear candles come in different forms like the ones I use, cotton or Muslim cloth covered in paraffin wax. There are bees wax candles but those are harder to work with, they are much softer. Then there are the candles infused with essential oils. I use different ones on occasion. There is sage, lavender, eucalyptus, ylang ylang, tea tree and so many more. If you are candling due to sinus or nasal blockage, try using a peppermint or eucalyptus . . . . very good for clearing those areas.

E—ENERGY

Energy is in everything and everywhere. Some forms of energy can be seen like us and the world we live in. Other type of energy is from God, angels, guides, loved ones in spirit and the energy within our bodies. Now I won't go into the scientific part of energy because that is just way beyond me, protons, neutrons and atoms . . . oh my! What I am going to write about here is the energy I work with.

The healing work I do for clients is all based on energy. My energy work is Reiki, Theta. Chakras, Crystals and Soul work. I use whatever I need to help my client. Some people come in to see me specifically for one modality or another, but I tend to add a little of the other modalities to it. Each modality works in a different way but they still all work the person's energy.

I'm sure you have noticed when you're not feeling yourself. Sometimes you just feel off, not right, no energy, sluggish, feeling down for no reason or out of sorts. Well your energy is off. This can be caused from physical illness, emotional distress or mental anguish. Then you have your days when you are feeling uplifted, energetic, happy, healthy, loving, joyful and so on. This means your energy is in alignment. Your body, mind and soul are in balance. Having balance is not always easy but you have to try and push yourself to be in a good state of balance. There has to be a happy medium of lows and highs.

Energy can be felt by anyone. Have you ever stepped into a crowded room and get introduced to someone only to have this feeling of needing to step away from that person? Well you are feeling there negative energy. Same if you meet someone who is of high positive energy. They give you the feeling of wow what a great person, I like them. When you are picking up energies from others you feel it right in your solar plexus. The chakra right above your belly button. That is your energy center. This is where you feel that sick to your stomach feeling when things are not good. Think about the last time you were talking with someone who was nothing but drama and negativity. How did you feel? I can bet that you felt drained. People who are negative will drain the energy right out of you. So remember to ALWAYS protect yourself. You never know who might run into. We will talk about ways of protecting yourself throughout this book. Now on the other hand, positive energy can be felt not only in your solar plexus but in your heart as well. You walk away from these people or situations feeling wonderful.

As I said earlier, energy is in everything. Did you ever pick up a crystal or stone, close your eyes and feel it's energy or vibration? The vibrations can be slight or very heavy. Intuitive's use this method to do readings for people. It is called psychometry. They can hold an object that belonged to your passed loved one and read it's energy. Usually these items are something that the person when here on earth had on their person like a ring, necklace, bracelet and so on. When the intuitive holds the object, they pick up information from it. Maybe who that person was, what they looked like, where they were from, their age, what they passed from and so on. Try this with a friend. Exchange items and do a reading for each other. Hold the object for a bit and just say to yourself "what do I feel when I hold this". Be patient with yourself if you don't feel anything right away. It takes practice. Intuitives may also like to hold your hands as well to read you. Many use that type of practice, this way they pick up your energy and the energy around you, and then the messages come through.

Energy is a major factor in our lives. It is everywhere and in everything. Practice feeling energy everyday. Try this. Hug a tree. Now your probably saying "what"? It's true. Try hugging a tree. When you hug or even place your hands on a tree, you can feel its energy. Take your time, don't just touch it and let go. Leave your hands there for a bit and close your eyes and just feel. Pay attention to your hands and you will feel the energy vibration. I tell my clients all the time that when they feel down to go outside and take three deep breaths. The energy from outdoors is so powerful. It will calm you right down. The ocean is another wonderful place to receive healthy positive energy. If you are lucky enough to live near the ocean, go there and find a spot that you feel comfortable in and just close your eyes, take three deep breaths and just be. Listen to the ocean waves, smell the salt air and feel the energy. You will not be disappointed. I live near the ocean and when I go it just gives me a huge feeling of peace and serenity.

Here is another exercise for you to try with a friend. Start by facing each other. The put your hands up to face your partner, palms facing each other not touching. After just a few seconds you should be able to feel each other's energy. If you don't, keep at it for a while longer until you do. Now once you feel each other's energy, pull your hands back a bit then back to where they were. Keep doing this and you will feel the energy expanding every time you pull your hands back away from theirs. What you have created is an energy ball. It is really fun to do and you can do this alone as well. Just face your palms and pull palms away and back like a swing away and swing to each other. Now you should be able to feel a energy ball between the palms of your hands. The longer you do and the further out you bring your hands the larger the energy ball gets. Then you can start to move your hand around the energy ball and feel the circumference of it. This is fun way of playing with energy. Practice and then you can move on to feeling energy with other things.

Auras are another way to sense energy. We all have an aura that extends out from our bodies and has many different colors just like our chakras. Some intuitives can see people's auras. They can read your energy by seeing your aura and if there is any tears or discoloration in it. When you have this it means that your energy is off due to some kind of imbalance. I don't see full auras but I can look at someone and see a color around them. I do see chakra color when I do Reiki. During Reiki I can check someone's aura to see if it extending out enough from the body. A person's aura should be at least 8-9 inches out from the body. When it is low and I do Reiki, after the session I recheck it and the aura is back up to where it should be.

You can check your own aura to see if your energy is up or down. Sit in a chair and place your hand with palm side facing down about one foot above your thigh and slowly allow your hand to come down until you feel a resistance. This may take a few tries before you feel it. If your energy is good you hand should stop about 8-9 inches above your thigh. If your energy is low then your hand will feel the energy at a much lower space. If your energy is low then consider having Reiki done, get a massage or find some kind of energy work that feels good to you.

Do everything you can to keep your energy up on a daily basis. Read a uplifting book, watch a funny movie, do things you enjoy, keep positive people in your life, meditate, use positive affirmations and always let go of what no longer serves you. Life is meant to be joyous, so when you run into a speed bump, deal with it and let it go. Always move forward.

You will never get anywhere moving backwards or standing still. Stay positive my friends and feel the love from within and from everyone and everything . . . it is yours for the taking.

Affirmations: My energy is always up.
                 I only choose things are good for my energy.

E—EMOTIONAL DISTRESS

Emotional distress can lead to physical ailments. It is my belief that when we get sick it is because we are not balanced emotionally and mentally. I also believe that stress is the biggest culprit today. We are put under so much pressure to do more and go faster. This stress comes from family, friends, work and ourselves. When stress builds up to much the body reacts. Our bodies can only take so much before it breaks down and gets physically ill. The physical illness can be anything from the sniffles to disease.

What is disease? Disease is an unbalance or break in the ease of the body. So there for it is referred to as dis-ease. When you get sick or feel rundown, look at what is going on in your life. Are there stresses, drama, worry or you haven't slowed down? Our bodies talk to us all the time and when something is off it lets us know. We have to learn to listen to it. We all get these signs from our bodies. You may feel a sniffle coming on, an ache, a pain, a headache and so on. What is your body telling you? When we have our emotions in check we are healthy. When we start with negative emotions like stress, anger, repressed trauma, worry, fear, mistrust, lack of confidence, lacking selfesteem, living in drama and so much more our bodies will be in dis-ease.

Here are some examples of physical illness connected to emotional distress. I am giving you a list of what I feel are the biggest one's today.

Headache	Inability to resolve emotional upsets Feelings of inner pressure working on you
Shoulders (Right) (Left) (Both)	Worry about finances Worry about family Feeling like the world is on your shoulders

Liver	Holding anger
Hips	Fear of making decisions Nothing to look forward to
Legs	Fear of moving forward Fear of change
Acne	Feelings of guilt Self-rejection
Allergies	Suppressed weeping Denying own power
Sinus	Being irritated by someone close to you
Rash	Being irritated by someone/something Unable to flow with life
Back problems	Feeling no support
Upper back	Feelings of frustration
Middle back	Guilt/lack of self esteem
Lower back	Feels unsupported financially Relationships that hurt
Insomnia	Tension in life Fear, anxiety, deep seeded grief
Postnasal drip	Inner grief Crying on the inside
Addictions	Distorted memory in the DNA Disproval of self Feeling a void in the soul
Ankles	Fear of failure
Anxiety	Feels boxed in Feels helpless to affect change
Colds	Unkind feeling towards someone Confusion in our life
Cold Sores	Inability to express anger
Deafness	Not wanting to hear what is said. Wanting to be isolated.

Eczema	Over sensitive Unresolved hurt feelings
Eyes (near sighted) (far sighted)	Not wanting to see what's ahead for you Not seeing what is right in front of you
Overweight	Feel a need for protection Hidden anger Resistance to forgiving Insecurity
Feet	Not liking the direction you are going in
Heart	Violating the laws of love Feelings of resentment/hurt Upsetting family problems
Knee problems	Inability to be flexible Stubborn/wants own way Ego gets in the way
Laryngitis	Fears voicing opinions Repressed emotions and fears
Lungs	Feelings of grief Not feeling approval from others
Memory (Lack of)	Don't feel valued Feels others not interested in what you know
Nail Biting	Unfulfilled desires Frustration Spiteful towards parents
Neck Problems	Moving under pressure Wanting to let feelings out but don't
Nose (blocked) (runny) (stuffy)	Not enjoying life Crying on the inside/wanting help Not accepting your worth Unwilling to just be yourself
Pimples	Unresolved frustrations Hidden anger surfacing

Shingles	Fears things won't work the way you want Ongoing tension concerning a situation
Stomach	Fears new ideas Lack of affection
Under Weight	Worries/fears Distrusting life
Varicose Veins	Pronounced tension Feeling over burdened
Warts	Not seeing the beauty in life Feelings of hate
Wrist	Holding onto old beliefs about life/self Imbalance in giving and receiving

Now this is a partial list, but I wanted you to see how the emotions carry over to the physical body. You may even connect with some of these that you just read. Once you recognize what is causing your physical illness you can work on the issue at hand and change what needs to be changed so you can be healthy and happy.

Use affirmations to change the way you think. Turn that negative into a positive. Let go of what no longer serves you. If someone is not a good fit for you're highest needs then maybe it is time to let that person go. Find situations and people who will benefit you and your life so that you can be happy and healthy!

You may thinking that you do know what is wrong but wonder how to fix it. There are many different ways to do this. Positive affirmations, like I just stated, Reiki to release emotional distress and pain/discomfort, Theta healing to change belief systems, or Hypnosis to release and let go of the old and create change.

Something else I wish to bring to your attention is that never claim an illness as your own. What I mean is, never say "My Cancer", "My Headache", "My Cold" and so on. When you do this you are claiming it as your own. Your body owns it. Whatever the mind thinks the body follows. So when you say "My Pain" for example, the mind is telling the body that it belongs there and don't let go. You want to refer to it as "This Pain" and then say a positive affirmation like" My body is healthy and moves with ease". So when you act and talk positive the mind will let the body know that what you are referring to does not belong and the statement of health is what is going to set in.

Keep those negative thoughts and words out of your head and your vocabulary. If you catch yourself saying something negative, just say cancel, cancel, cancel and replace it with a positive thought or word(s). To learn more about emotional distress, I recommend a book called "Feelings Buried Alive Never Die" by Karol K. Truman. This is an awesome book that has taught me a lot and I also use as a guide when working with my clients and students. Her book goes into more detail than I can mention here. It really gets into emotions, illness, how to change the way we speak and think. So yes we can change our negative behaviors if we WANT to! It is a choice and the choice is yours.

Affirmation: I am a healthy positive person.
I change my old ways easily and quickly.
I now release anything/anyone that no longer serves me.

F—FAITH

Faith is having trust in what or whom you believe in. Faith has many aspects, such as faith in God, religious faith, faith in yourself or someone. Today many people have a great faith in God. They don't necessarily have a religious faith but have a faith and belief in God.

For me, I was raised Catholic but today I no longer practice. I let go of my religious faith because many of the Catholic churches rules and regulations I find to be hypocritical. They like to change the rules as they go along and to suit them. They have given me many reasons to walk away. Today I call myself Spiritual. I believe in God, Jesus, Mother Mary, the Angels and much more. I know that I can talk to God from where ever I am. I don't need this huge building with gold and fine linens to talk to God. God is everywhere.

I know in my heart that we all need to go with what feels right to us. I'm sure many of you were brought up with a faith and maybe now are questioning it. Certain things don't feel right to you anymore. I say go with your heart and what feels right. Then you have to let go of the fear that you will be condemned for going against what you were taught to believe.

Believe me I am not picking on religion here and I am very open to what people feel is right for them, but there are religions out there that use scare tactics to make sure that people stay in church instead of preaching that God is all loving and really giving people a reason to want to stay. They also tell you that if you don't do this or that you will go to hell and God will judge you. The only hell there is, is the one that we create for ourselves. Life can be great or life can be hell. It's up to you. Instead they should be telling everyone that God is an all Loving God, who does not judge and loves us unconditionally. I have faith that God loves each and every one of us and the only judgment comes from ourselves. I am not a religious expert, so I am not going to elaborate on them. The only thing

I will write of is my own experiences that I have had and what I believe in now. I just ask that you go within and see and feel what is right for you. True faith comes from the heart and when your heart is open, you have God.

Faith has many other meanings. You may have faith that rain will hold off so you can have an outdoor activity. Maybe you have faith that there is a significant other out there somewhere for you. Having this kind of faith is a trust and belief that it will happen. This is a great positive way to be. This is how we attract what it is that we want. I'm sure many of you have heard of or read the book called "Law Of Attraction". You put it out there to the universe what it is you want with the full belief that you will receive it and you do. This is a great thing that I will touch on more, later in the book.

Many times in life we lose our faith. Whether it be in God or ourselves. We go through those bumps in the road in life and feel as though we let ourselves down or let god down. Then there are those times when you feel like God has let you down and not answered your prayers. Well let me reassure you that God does hear every single prayer and he does help us. Unfortunately we don't always hear or feel the answers. We go through these rough patches in life to learn for our soul. These are issues we need to go through to learn and grow spiritually. What you have to remember is that we go through these for a reason and no matter how big or small, we have to hold onto our faith and believe that all will be well. Sometimes things happen to us because we are moving off of our path. Remember that God will always get us through. The more you keep the faith the easier it will be to go through the rough patches and come out the other side a better person.

Never focus on the bad part of any situation. With every bad there is a good. That is what you need to focus on. Turn things around and be positive. Think of what you learned from your situation and be sure not to go there again. Learn the lesson the first time. Some tend to repeat the same thing over and over and their soul cannot progress if it doesn't learn. I have talked with many people who go through issues or disease and they tell me how much better everything is when they stay positive. They keep their faith that everything will be and is better. Some have told me that if they hadn't gone through whatever situation they had, they would not be where they are today and not feel the importance in life. Like I said before, everything happens for a reason. Take the lesson and move forward. Keep the faith that everything will be OK.

Affirmation: I have faith that all is well.
I trust that there is a higher power to help me.
I only think and speak in a positive way.

F—FEAR

Fear is an emotion that comes directly from the ego. We all have fear to a certain extent. Learning to overcome the fear is the challenge. Many people live in fear and this is not healthy. There are so many opportunities out there for us, but we tend to listen to our ego and never go for it. Why because we let that ego take over and convince us that we are not good enough or capable of doing something. We need to let go of the fear and go with our hearts that are NEVER wrong.

Fear develops because others either have told us that we can't do something, we are not good enough or we worry about what everyone else thinks, don't trust that we are right or don't have the faith we need to move forward with a decision. We all have fear within us which is a natural human emotion that we do need at times, like when we something scares us (accident, close call, worry about family). We do need and have fear to an extent, but you cannot let fear take over. This is when we hold ourselves back from moving forward and then worry ourselves to the point of panic or anxiety. This is ego-based fear.

I have worked with many clients that are looking for guidance and when I tell them to let go of the fear and just go for it and they have the support of god and the Angels. They right away say "I don't think I can do that and what If"? That little phrase "what if" is just fear and excuses of why not to move forward. We tend to hold ourselves back too much. I learned how to let go of fear. Believe me I still get fearful at times but the difference now is I recognize it right away and say "the heck with it I am just going to do it". I let go of the fear and move forward. This doesn't happen overnight. It took me time and practice to reach this point. Now I find myself saying that if I am wrong, so what. Can't be right all the time. Lesson learned and I move on. I also learned to trust my gut. Many times I would get that gut feeling and go against it and then be so upset that I didn't listen.

When I opened my healing center with my sister, I had moments when my intuition was really starting to flow. I would stay in the ego and think I can't tell this person anything, what if I am wrong? Well after a little while I would get messages from my Angels and they would say to me, "tell them what they need to hear that is why we give you the information". Then I thought to myself, then I will and if I'm wrong so what, I have to trust and let go of the fear. Then to my amazement, I would tell them what I received and I was right. The Angels were giving me the right information. It was just fear. I learned to let go and move forward with love, trust and faith.

Today I continue to give messages and never worry because I know and have the confidence I need to do my healings and readings. I know the information will come through. I faced my fear and won.

Another example of fear that I once had was when I was asked to speak in from of a women's cancer group about Reiki. I wanted to do it but at the same time I was fearful that I would say the wrong thing or stutter the words. I had never spoke in public before. I heard in my head, you have to face your fear and you will be fine. So I said yes. I was nervous on that day but I trusted that all would go well. So I called in my Angels right before my talk and I went in and said everything I needed to say and even had time to do a 10 meditation with them, everyone loved it. The person who leads the group told me how great I did and that she would love to have me back again. I said yes and then explained to her how nervous I was and that I have never spoken in public before and she said that she didn't even notice. She was so sure I had done this before.

I still do talks at the hospital on occasion. In fact I think the Angels really challenged me a few years ago when I was asked to talk to all the social workers at the hospital. They were doing a presentation on alternative therapies and ask me to talk about Reiki, so I said yes. How many social workers can there be, right? Well to my surprise that morning about 40 or more social workers showed up. Big difference from a cancer group of about 8-10. Then one of the social workers told me that there are some skeptics in the room but not to worry. Well easy for her to say. Now I'm worrying. I sat down and right next to me was a skeptic. Oh boy now what? Well I called on my Angels again to keep me calm and help me do what I was there to do. I did it and I did it great! Many of the people there that day told me how informative I was and that they were grateful that I was there to talk with them. You just have to trust and let go of the fear. I survived you can too. No matter what you set out to do.

Fear can be anything from a fear of bugs, heights, flying, animals, public speaking, starting something new, opening a business and so much more. How do you know how you will do unless you try? Some fears are carried over from a past life. Such as lets say you have never been afraid of bugs then one day you are suddenly terrified of bugs. What happened there is in a past life at a specific time in your life then; you experienced a terrifying moment with bugs. You know have past life cell memory that is coming though in this life at the same time as your past life. This doesn't happen with everyone, but it can happen to some. Hypnosis can help to release these past life issues that were carried over by doing regression. In regression I tell the subconscious mind to let go of the issue that was in your past life and you can now move forward in this life clear of old cell memory. Also you can ask the Angels to help you to release past life issues that you may have carried over into this life.

When you have fear ask Archangel Michael to help you to release fears, doubts and what no longer serves you. He is the Angel that also gives you protection, strength and courage. I refer to him as the "Big Guy". I call on him all the time. Archangel Raphael is the other one to call in. He can help you to heal emotionally so you can change old belief systems and have him replace that with positive healing energy.

Here is a meditation that you can use to release fears. First find a quiet place to sit comfortable. Close your eyes and take three deep breaths so you can relax. Now visualize these two beautiful Angels and see their colors of royal blue (Michael) and emerald green (Raphael). Ask Archangel Michael to us his spiritual vacuum to vacuum away your fear about _____. See it being sucked away as a dark mist going right up into his vacuum. Then ask Archangel Raphael to send his healing energy down though the crown of your head and throughout your whole body all the way to your toes, filling you with healing energy and replacing what was taken away with positive energy. Feel or sense the energy as it moves through you. Thank them for helping you. Now bring your awareness back and open your eyes.

Keep practicing this meditation until you feel that your fear is gone. Only work on one fear at a time. The Angels are always there to help us, all you have to do is ask. If you find that you are having a tough time releasing your fear(s) then you may need a little help with one of the modalities I mentioned earlier. Live life to the fullest. Let go of what no longer serves you, live in the moment, always move forward and have love in your heart.

Affirmation: I have the courage and strength to do anything I set out to do. I now release my fears and move forward with ease.

F—FORGIVENESS

Forgiveness is the ability to let go of a wrong that was done or said against you or anyone else. Forgiveness has got to be the hardest thing to do. Most people tend to hold onto the wrongs that others have done against them. Some feel that those people should suffer for what they have done. Eye for an eye or you hurt me now I'm going to hurt you. Well this is not right. Remember when we were children, our parents would say two wrongs don't make a right. They were right. Be the bigger person, let it go and forgive.

When someone does something wrong against you, know that they are living in the ego with no love. They may be living a life where all they know is selfishness, close minded, lack of love and so on. They may have been raised that way and don't know anything else. To you they have hurt you by being a mean unloving person. Before you lose control, you have to stop and forgive this person because people like that have an underlying reason for acting this way. Not that I am condoning this believe me but we have to look at it with wonder of why this person acts the way they do.

We are all a spark of the Divine and that is what we have to remember. We all need to let go of the anger and live in the divine spark of love. As far as the other person, they will have to find on their own. We can pray for them in hopes that they too find that spark of love and change for the better.

Now I know that there are things out there that are extreme and severe like murder, rape, child molestation and the like. How do we forgive these types of people? It is not easy, but they too need to be forgiven. You will not forget, but you need to forgive. Going through something like this is like a severe grief of a loved one. You think that you will never get over it, but you do and will. These people need to be forgiven. Not for them but for yourself. If you hold onto the anger from whatever happened, you will never be able to move forward. It will consume you and eat you up inside.

This is when you have to trust that Karma will come into play and the universe will take care of it.

Forgiveness can be done face to face. Let that other person know you forgive them. Communication is so important! Discuss what ever happened between the two of you and forgive, let go and move on. Now if you can't talk to the person face to face either because they refuse to talk or you don't know where they are, you can still forgive. You can do this by saying to yourself that you forgive them and let it go. You can also meditate where you see that person and see yourself talking with them, forgiving them. Then lastly you can always call on Archangel Michael to help you to forgive and let go of the situation with this person and feel Archangel Michael around you and pulling this weight off your shoulders.

What to do when the person you need to forgive has passed away? Don't think that just because someone has passed that the emotions from the situation has gone with them. You still need to forgive them. I feel that the best way to do this is by writing that person a letter. It may sound silly but it works. Write a letter stating everything you ever wanted to say to them, get it all out and forgive them! You can then place it in an envelope and put it somewhere in a drawer or you can burn it (safely) with the intention that the smoke is carrying it up to heaven. Either way is fine. Just know that the person you wrote to heard your words and accepts them. You can also just talk out loud to them, they can hear you too. Some people feel silly just talking out loud so if you feel this way then write the letter.

Self-forgiveness is another big one! We will at times forgive others before we forgive ourselves. Self—forgiveness is very important. We go through so many things in life that we regret, feel guilty about or feel we could have done better. We tend to live in the shoulda, coulda, woulda, only if, what if and so on. This is living in the past and holding guilt about yourself. If you stay there you will never move forward. Whatever happened, happened. It can't be changed. You just have to accept it and forgive yourself. I tell my clients all the time, if you worry about it, does it change anything? The answer is always NO. Forgiveness is the same. If you hold onto the guilt about your past, does it change anything? The answer again is no. You cannot change the past. Please just forgive yourself, let it go and realize that it (whatever it was) was a life lesson and you take what you learned and move forward. We all have life lessons to learn in life and when things don't go the way we planned, know there is a reason why.

You just need to let go of the guilt and stop thinking it was your fault that things went wrong. Forgive yourself and move on.

Here is an example. My husband had gone to college for pharmacy. Unfortunately things didn't go the way he planned and he left college. He would beat himself up and say, "I should have applied myself more, I should have done better". I told him that he needed to let that go and that he can't change the past. I then reminded him that if things did work out at school he would have never met me. He would have gone in a different direction. Everything happens for a reason. You see my husband ended up working at the same place as my father and as time went by my father asked him if he would be interested in meeting me (Dad was a match maker)? So he agreed and gave his phone number to my father and visa versa. So we began to talk on the phone, then started dating and the rest is history. We are married 12 years now and have 3 children. So it is true, everything happens for a reason and the way it should be.

Parents need to forgive themselves too. They tend to blame themselves for how their children turn out. First thing they say is "where did I do wrong"? Your children have their own lives to live. As a parent is it your job to be there life teacher. It is up to them to take those lessons you taught and go with it. If they don't it is not your fault. Forgive yourself and let it go. They will have to learn their own lessons just as we did and continue to do. You cannot blame yourself for what others do. Just give your children love and compassion then step back from the situation as it is theirs not yours. Unless they finally see the light and truly want your help, then by all means help. Use your best judgment, you will know what to do and when.

Affirmation: I now forgive _____ for all past hurts and move forward.
I now forgive myself for _____.
I am now forgiven and have a love in my heart. I now live in the present and let go of the past.

FORGIVENESS + LOVE = HARMONY

G—GRATITUDE

Gratitude is giving thanks for what we have and what we receive everyday, no matter how big or how small. There are those who replace gratitude with granted. Meaning we still take so many things for granted. We assume that people and things will be there for us forever. We forget to have gratitude. I give thanks everyday. When I pray, I thank God for waking up in the morning, having another day to learn, love, and for him.

Unfortunately some people only focus on what they don't have. That is a negative feeling to have. I tell my clients that they have to let that go and focus on what they do have like a roof over their head, food, family, friends, health and so on. Some just focus on the bad relationship, rotten job, the old car that works badly, the bills that just keep piling up and the kids who don't listen. I teach them how to turn that negative thinking around and turn it into grateful positive statements.

I am grateful for a relationship full of love.

I am grateful for a job that pays me well so that I can live comfortable.

I am grateful for a car that gets me everywhere I need to go.

I am grateful for the financial flow that comes to me every day.

I am grateful for my children who are true gifts from God.

See how you can turn things around. Focus on the positive. Even if in the moment one or all of these are not true, still say it until it is true. The more you do it, the more you will be grateful for many things in your life. One of my teachers told me. Fake it until you make it. Remember the mind will follow what you tell it. So keep a positive attitude, affirm daily and watch as life turns around to a more positive lifestyle. The choice is yours. Live in the "poor me" attitude or put your foot down and make those changes.

How many of you are in a relationship and in the beginning would show your other half that you love them deeply and always show them affection. Then as time goes by you start to show less and less. We start taking them for granted. What happens is time goes by and we just take it for granted that the other person knows we love them and we appreciate what they do for us. I don't know about you but I still love to hear I Love You from my husband. He even says thank you for very little thing I do. I do the same for him. We really need to remember to always show love and gratitude.

When we don't show this to others, the relationship will not last and if it does it won't be a happy one. Another aspect to look at is the possibility of losing that person in death and never really showing them your gratitude. Now you not only feel grief but now you feel guilt. You now wish you had said more, tell them how much you love them and really told them how much you appreciated them. So in other words don't put off till tomorrow what you can do today. Always show your love and gratitude every day because we never know which day will be our last.

Do this for everyone and everything in your life. You need to be grateful. I don't care how bad things seem to be, there is always something good about it. Always focus on the good and the bad just seems to be not so bad after all.

Even the Law of Attraction, which many books have been written about, tells us that when we want to attract something into our lives we have to act as if it already is. We have to be grateful for it even though we don't have it yet. Let's say you are trying to attract a new job, here is what you need to say: I am <u>Grateful Now</u> That I have a job that is <u>(fill in your dream job description)</u>, pays me $_____ per hour, has perfect hours for me and has co-workers that are positive. You will attract that job. The other thing is to hold that positive belief and trust that it is coming to you. If you only say the affirmation and keep the negative mindset, you will not get it.

Here is a gratitude challenge for you. Everyday write down just 10 things you are grateful for. At first you may find this difficult, but as the days go by you will find it to be much easier and will start noticing even the small things in life that you should be grateful for. Show gratitude from the smallest things to the larger things. Here is a list of things you could be grateful for.

I AM GRATEFUL FOR:

My husband, partner, boy/girl friend
My children, grandchildren
A beautiful place to live
A car that takes me where I need to go
A great job that pays me well
My friends/family
The person who held the door open for me
The driver that let me pass first
The food I eat
Guidance from God and the Angels
The person who picked up the object I
Dropped.
My teacher/mentor
The wonderful weather we had today
All the blessings in my life
The person who bought me a coffee today
The person who said thank you

Practice gratitude every day and you will see how your life becomes more positive when you spend more time looking at the good things in life.

Affirmations: I am Grateful today.
I am now grateful for _____.
Gratitude is always part of my life.

G—GUILT

Guilt is something we all feel from time to time. The guilt that I am going to talk about is when we are being taken advantage of. I have talked with so many people who tell me that they do this that and the other for everyone. When I ask them when they take time for themselves, they say they don't have time for themselves and they are way to busy. I proceed to explain that they need to do things for themselves and take time to relax. That's when I hear "well I feel bad if I say no to them". This is called having guilt.

When I ask a client. "Who is at the top of your priority list? They never say themselves. The list everything or everyone but not them. You need to put yourself at the top of your list. It is not a selfish thing, but if you don't take care of your needs, you're not going to be able to take care of everything/everyone else. You will suffer burn out at some point. Believe me it is good to help others but there are limits.

You have those who expect you to help them all the time and not allow you time for their needs. There is a simple solution to this problem . . . SAY NO! You know it really is ok to say this little two-letter word. Many people feel that they just can't say no to others. They feel it is wrong and if they do . . . here comes the guilt. I don't mean for you to be inconsiderate, but sometimes we just have to say no and that's ok. All you have to tell the other person is "I would love to help you but at this time I really can't, but if you need me at another time feel free to ask". If the other person is a good person, they will understand, if they don't then they are taking advantage of you. When you start practicing the art of saying no, you will lose that guilty feeling.

Another guilt trip we put on ourselves is thinking our husband and children can't live without us. I had wanted to do classes and do things with my friends but I would feel guilty. I would say to myself that I couldn't go because I need to stay home and take care of them. What would my husband think? In all reality it turned out that they didn't even mind that I would go out and have fun at times. I was the one that was holding myself back. When I first decided to go out and things for me, I felt really guilty but I went anyway. I then came to realize that there was nothing to feel guilty about and that they did survive without me. You see that was how I was raised, to take care of my husband and children. It was a belief system I needed to change and I did.

Other ways we feel guilt is when someone close to us is in a bad mood or upset about something and the first thing we think is . . . what did I do? Well unless you intentionally did something, why are you feeling guilty? I used to do that. If my husband was upset about something, right away I think I did something and he is mad at me. Unless you ask what is wrong, you don't know. You need to let go of the guilt. You are placing it the on purpose without even knowing what is wrong. I think we all do this at one point or another because we feel we have to please everyone all the time and when those people are not happy, it must be our fault. First you need to ask what is wrong and then allow them to say it. If they don't want to talk, that's ok. They will talk when they are ready. Then you need to let it go. When they do decide to open up, just be there for them and help if they want it.

How many people do you know who got divorced or separated and the first thing they say is "what did I do"? We first add guilt then sit there and let our ego do the talking. What could I have done better? Did I put enough into the relationship? It must be my fault. You know, sometimes relationships just end. They really do. It could be that your just not compatible. Maybe you both rushed into the relationship too quickly. Maybe now that you really got to know each other, you or the other person decides that the other is not really what they were looking for in a relationship. Sometimes we just want different things in life and that is ok. Then we just have to accept that and move on.

What about abusive relationships? How many spouses are abused physically, mentally, emotionally or sexually? When this happens they believe that it is their fault and they must of done something wrong and deserve it. THIS IS NOT SO! Understand right now that when you are in this kind of relationship, you need to get out! It is not your fault. Usually people who do the abuse are looking for power and control. They look for this because for some reason they feel inadequate so they make others feel and look bad so they themselves can look better. All they are is a grown up bully. Some of these abusers unfortunately do this because they were raised in the same setting. Instead of going the opposite way to better themselves, they just follow along with what they had growing up. Do not let yourself feel guilty about this. It is not your fault and please stop making excuses for that person. No one on Gods green earth deserves this type of treatment. If you or someone you know is going through this situation, get out now and get some help. Also use the information you read so far from this book. Call in your Angels. They will help you and give you strength and courage.

Children are another aspect that we bring guilt into. We get married or not, have children, spend 18 years raising them, teaching them values and morals and then they don't turn out the way we planned. Here comes the guilt. "Where did I go wrong, it's all my fault"? You know we all do our best to raise our children to the best to our ability. We gave them everything they needed in life. We taught them everything we know. Showed them the way. It is up to them to take the lessons and go with it. It is their choice. It is not your fault. I tell my clients it is like a teacher in school who does her lessons everyday and yet a student still continues to fail. Well she/he can only do so much. It is up to the students to take the lessons and apply themselves so they can pass the class. It is not your fault. You can do everything in your power to make that child learn and if they don't want to, what can you do? This could be their personality. This could also be a life's lesson for them. Whatever their age.

Other parents tend to do everything for their children and then the child becomes an adult expecting that mom and dad will always be there to support them and you decide that it is time for them to fend for themselves. So you decide to cut ties and tell your child they have to start supporting themselves. This is where tough love comes in. Now your child probably won't like this but it is best for them so they can stop taking advantage of you and learns how to deal with things themselves. Now your probably going to feel guilty, don't. You know in your heart you did the right thing. I always say go with your heart. The heart is never wrong. This is a lesson for you too. They need to learn independence and you need to learn to let go.

WE all go through many things in life that we feel guilty about. You have to look at the situation and see if there is a reason to feel guilty. Did you go with your ego or did you go with your heart. So please let go of the guilt. We are all beautiful beings of light and if your intensions are loving, good and from the heart, then you can let it go and live in the light.

Affirmation: I now release all guilt to God and only feel the love and light.
I see every situation through the eyes of God.

G—GOD

God is the creator of all that is. This is my belief and I'm sure the belief of many of you. It is today considered the touchiest subject to discuss. Many are afraid to mention God because they might offend someone. Then you have those who want to take God out of everything, our money (In god we trust) and the pledge of allegiance (Under God). I know in my heart that if it weren't for God, nothing would be here or be possible.

Religions preach about God, no matter what name they choose to call him. Unless you are atheist and you don't even believe in God. God is in everything and is everywhere. God is an all-loving God and his love is unconditional. God never judges us. To him/her we are perfect. We are the only ones who can judge ourselves. God is not a man as many would think but a source of love and light energy that is so great, none of us could ever comprehend. God is not male or female, but is made up of both male and female energy. I have come to believe through many books and teachings that God is male energy, which is intellect, and female energy, which is emotion. When I pray I always say Dear Father and Mother God. Think about it. When you check the bible, it does say, "we will make them (Adam & Eve) in the likeness if us" . . . not me. Which shows there is a duality there? You have to have both energies to have balance in the mind, body and soul. Everyone has both energies. In fact your right side is male and your left side is female.

Know that as you continue to read on, I will just write God and not Mother/Father God. Just for the sake of less writing, but I do mean both when I refer to God. Father God is all energy and intellect. He does not hold a form such as a human body, but is pure energy and light. He also is the one who sends his Angels down here to earth to help us. Mother God is the source that acts. She can and has manifested before us. She will make herself known to us in many different ways when we need her most. Many believe that the Blessed Mother was a manifestation of Mother God and so was the Lady of Lourdes. There have been so many accounts of seeing visions of Mother God throughout the years. If you have noticed every time there is a vision of the Mother God/Mother Mary, there is always a great message that she brings. I also believe that when you see these images it is a reminder to keep God in our hearts and souls. It is also a message to keep peace, harmony and love throughout the world.

This also applies to the stories of Jesus manifesting in images. Again it is a reminder to let go of the hate, the fighting, anger and judgment. We All need to take these messages, spread them around and help to make changes in this world we live in. You may be saying "how can I change the world"? All you have to do is live in love and pray that the love spread throughout the world. Everyone one positive intention brings us closer to peace . . . so imagine if we all did this, how magnified it would be. Negative energy would make a shift to a more positive energy. So when you say your prayers, please ask for peace to surround our beautiful earth and everyone in it, then visualize a pink light around the globe, infusing the earth and people with loving energy.

God is an all loving God. He/She loves us unconditionally no matter what we do in life, good or bad. We are ALL his/her children. God knows that we are all here to learn and as with any learning process we are going to make some mistakes. God does not judge us either. Some religions will tell in one sentence that God does not judge and in the next sentence says that if you do wrong, God will condemn you to Hell. Please people, make up your mind, which is it? I find this very hypocritical. I will mention the Catholic religion for example (only because I was Catholic). Catholics have always had the rule of no meat on Friday during lent. Ok that sounds reasonable. Well a few years ago, St. Patrick's Day landed on a Friday. So now the church decides that it is ok to eat meat on this Friday and you won't go to Hell for it. Well if I remember correctly, we were always told that if we ate meat on Friday we would go to Hell. Now all these years sinners who did eat meat, passed away and then went to Hell, what happens to them? Does the church call them back and say "Oh it is ok to come to heaven now we changed our minds". To me this is all man made Rules, not God's rules. Man changes the rules so that it can suit them. One of the reasons I left the church.

I truly believe that religion is just using scare tactics to keep people in church. Maybe if they focused more on spreading the love and teaching of God being an all loving God, they would keep a lot more people in church who want to be there and don't feel scared and intimidated. I believe all lot of people are starting to see the truths for themselves. There are so many leaving churches, changing religions or just going with being spiritual, which is what I am. I don't believe I have to be in a huge building full of gold, marble and stain glass windows to talk to God. Isn't God everywhere and within each one of us? Yes he/she is.

Remember these are my opinions and I am very open to whatever people choose for themselves. I believe it is whatever works for you. It just doesn't work for me. Always go with what your heart is telling you, whether it is a certain religion, church or otherwise. If it makes you happy then do it.

Unfortunately I have had a few bad experiences with the church. Since I was a child, I did not like being in church. I didn't know why, but I just knew I didn't want to be there. It didn't feel good. Once I made my confirmation, I never went back until my husband and I were expecting our first child. Then I thought well maybe it would be a good idea to go back, good for all of us. So we attended church regularly. Then seventeen months later we had twin girls. We decided to have the girls baptized and set a date with the priest. This is when my faith in the church started to fall apart. The day of the baptism, we went to mass at 11:00am. During the mass our son was sitting quietly until the priest go to the sermon. My son made a couple of babbling noises, not loud at all. When to my shock the priest stopped talking, looked right at me and said I need you to leave, your son is disrupting my sermon and my people can't hear me. He did this out loud in front of the whole congregation. I was so embarrassed. At first I didn't think he was talking to me, but he was. So I grabbed the twins and my son and went to the basement of the church. I was so angry, I could not believe what had just happened. I've heard of people being thrown out of places before, but a church! Strike one.

A time before this episode of being thrown out of church, I was in mass with my son and a new priest came in to do mass as a guest. He was telling us that he was in one of those poor countries attending a monk's conference. He continued with a story of how the beggars would knock on the door asking for food. Here comes the shock . . . he said that he and the monks ate 3 times a day and when the beggars came he told them that no one there could help them or feed them. He said to us, "Well if we give up our food to feed one we would have to feed them all". I was so sick to my stomach. I don't know about you, but if I had to I could live on one meal a day to help a poor starving person. Strike two.

In 2009 I found out that the Catholic Diocese denounced Reiki. As you know I am a Reiki Master. They informed their parishioners o stay away from anyone who said they did Reiki, because their energy is not from God as they will claim, but energy from the devil. They continued to say that Reiki healings cannot be proven, which they have . . . sorry. They also said that the only healings that can take place other than medical is a natural or divine healing through the church. Well I would love to see them prove a divine healing, you can't. They even went as far as telling their people not to let us (reiki practitioners) touch them because we would only be hurting them with the devils energy. Really? I know firsthand that Reiki can do some amazing things for people. I have seen it happen right in my healing room. Now I have never claimed to fully heal people, but tell people there is a chance that Reiki can help improve many things for you. I don't know about anyone else but I haven't killed anyone yet with Reiki.

I truly feel it is a power thing with the church. I think they feel that they will lose their power of healing with their parishioners if there is someone else out there that can help just as much if not more. If we are all a part of God, then why can't we all do his work? Jesus did lying of hands, he healed many people. So why not you or me? After all Jesus was a human being just like us. We all have a natural born healing power within us, even if it is only a touch or a hug. If it brings healing to someone, then we are healers. Strike three.

This was the last straw! My sister and I planned a spiritual retreat in April 2011. We had people ready to go, all paid up and just counting down the days until we finally went. This was a catholic retreat center and in their ad it says ALL WELCOME. I called and told them what we were going to do at the retreat, meditation, breathwork, massage and Reiki (during down times). She said that was fine and she was happy that we would be attending their retreat center. Well only one week before the retreat we got a call. The woman said "I'm sorry but you are not allowed to hold your retreat here. Someone called the Bishop and said you were doing Reiki, so they want you out. Oh My God! Are you kidding me I said to her? I explained that the Reiki was only for my people and I was not promoting it in their center. She apologized and said if it was her decision she would have us there, but she couldn't go against the Bishop. Strike four . . . I AM OUT FOR GOOD! No more catholic church!

Luckily, I stayed faithful and asked my Angels to help us find a retreat center that could take us in a hurry. I told them it had to be within a hour or so from home and room for the 9 of us. Well by the next day, we had found a place that just happened to have 9 beds open and would love to have us there. We got it all together in one day and that's where we went and it was the best retreat ever! We are going back again in November 2011. Looking forward to future trips next spring and fall 2012.

As far as I'm concerned, I will never walk into a catholic church again unless it is a wedding or funeral. I explained to my husband that this is what I decided and he understood. He still attends church and that is his choice. He does it for the fact that he believes it is God's house and that is what he is there for, not the priest or the judgment. I can't be part of a religion that is judgmental, a hypocrite, discriminates and preaches love for all when they don't even show it themselves. God wouldn't do that to us.

If you feel the need to be part of a church, any church, then go for it. I just think you need to take what you want from it and leave the rest behind. Go with what feels right to you in your heart. I think people can have a religion and their own personal beliefs from outside the church. Remember we are all entitled to our own beliefs and opinions, respect everyone.

Affirmation: I always go with what feels right to my heart.
I hold God close to my heart and live through him daily.

H—HYPNOSIS

Hypnosis is a modality used to change a person's way of thinking and change behavior patterns. Most know about hypnosis for quitting smoking and losing weight which is the most popular reasons for seeing me. Hypnosis can be used for such more. I have clients that come to see me for anxiety, confidence, releasing negative patterns, fears, phobias and so much more. Past life regression is another part of hypnosis. People will have this done to let go of old negative patterns or fears. Many times these types of issues occur because we have carried them over from a past life.

Hypnosis is a very effective tool for people who are willing and ready to change their behavior or negative patterns. That is key, they have to be ready. Hypnosis will not work if the person is not willing and ready. You can't do hypnosis because your spouse, let's say want you make changes, you have to want it. Anything you want to do or change has to be up to you.

Hypnosis is done by the client lying down on the massage table, soft music in the back ground. Then I proceed to relax them with a relaxation meditation. Then I talk them down deeper and deeper into a hypnotic state. At this point the conscious mind goes to sleep as they say and the sub conscious mind is ready and willing to hear all the suggestions that I have for the person I am working with. People think that you are asleep, you are not. You are just so relaxed and your mind is waiting for the suggestions. You can still hear noises in the background, but it does not disturb you. You are still aware. It is nothing like stage hypnosis. I can't make you run around like a chicken.

I always fine tune the hypnotic suggestions according to the person's needs and habits. I have had great success with my clients. It has worked more often than not and if for some reason it doesn't work the first time, I will have them come back for a complimentary second session. Then there is usually success. Some people sometimes just need that extra reinforcement. There are those that hypnosis just won't work for them, for whatever reason. Then I offer them other suggestions of other modalities that might work for them. Just about every person who gets off my table tells me how relaxed they are and much lighter they feel. Like a load has been lifted.

Past life regression is done the same way as hypnosis. The difference is, instead of giving suggestions to change behavior; I bring them back through this life into their past life. There are a couple of reasons someone would want this done. One is to go back and see if there is something from the past life that was carried over into this life. Did you or someone you know ever suddenly become afraid of something they were never afraid of before? Well this could be because in their past life at the same time they are in this life that fear occurred. So now they feel this fear. Cell memory is the reason. Sometimes we do carry over some cell memory from that past life into our new lives.

Here is an example: I worked with a woman some time ago, who would feel like she was suffocating anytime her face was against something like a pillow or if she go a cold she would automatically feel like she was suffocating. So right away I felt it was a past life issue. So we proceeded to do the past life regression only to find out that in her past life at the same age she is at this time, someone had broken into her home and from behind covered her face with a rag and suffocated her. Then I explain to her while she was still under that she is no longer in that life and that she can let that memory go and move on in her life now, free of fear. After the session she told me how much better she felt and in the weeks after she said she no longer felt like she was suffocating.

Another example is when one of my twins was just turning two years old. My husband and I would take our three kids to the playground. Our daughter would always go up on the platform without an issue until one day right after she turned two; she had a fit and cried until I took her down. So that night once she fell asleep I whispered to her that the fear she was holding onto was from a past life and she is in a new life now and can let that old fear go. We went back to the playground and she climbed right up to the platform and continued to play without issue.

Reason two is just for curiosity sake. Some people just want to know who they were in a past life. I've done this before with clients. What happens is I take them back to the previous life and find out who they were. I ask questions like:

- Who are you?
- How old are you?
- Where do you live?
- What year is it?
- Are you married?
- Do you have kids?
- How did you pass?
- Ask for details of the scenery.
- What is your occupation?

It is very interesting to see who people were in their past life and how they lived. Ever notice someone who is really attached to something? Say someone who really loves, let's say, woodworking. It could be that in a past life they were a carpenter. Ever find yourself such good friend and feel like you really know them, you have similarities, and you feel more like connected souls instead of just friends. Well more than likely you both shared a past life together before and those feelings of closeness have carried over to this life. You both may have contacted to share a life together again.

So you see Hypnosis is a great tool to use to change behaviors, heal the body, mind and soul and to see yourself in your past life. Just be sure that you are ready for change and not because someone else wants you too.

Affirmation: I am now ready to change and heal for my well-being.

H—HOLISTIC HEALING

Holistic healing is a means of healing the body, mind and soul other than medical. Holistic healing can be done with one or more modalities that work with the energies within your body and bringing balance to your system. Depending on your needs, you may also use healthy supplements and herbs to treat your illness instead of traditional medicine. I'm not saying don't ever go to a doctor, because I believe that there are cases where you may need one. There are seriously critical issues that do require medical attention. There are many issues that can be fixed or healed through holistic means. There are also times when both can be used to help someone heal, holistic and medical. They complement each other very nicely.

I work with cancer patients on a regular basis. Giving them Reiki along with their medical treatment helps them so much. The medicine does its job while I do Reiki. The Reiki helps them to relax, removes anxiety and helps them with any pain and discomfort they may have. I would never expect them to leave their medical treatment, but adding Reiki is very good for them. I have read articles of people who have chosen to go completely holistic and they have healed 100% without medical treatment. This is a personal choice and a decision that needs to be thought out completely . . . it's called faith in God.

I think if people today would learn to let things go, reduce their stress and give up the drama, we would see less illness. Stress is the biggest culprit today with everyone having extra busy lives that we have today. You would think that with all of today's technology, things would be easier. Instead it just made us busier because with machines giving us more time we are filling that time with more stuff to do. Any

So many people today are running to the Doctor because of anxiety. Instead of finding ways to reduce their stress, they just get a pill from the Doctor to make it all better. What they don't realize is that the pills just mask the problem it doesn't fix it. I'm sure there are some out there that have mental illness and need medication, but the rest of the people can help themselves through other means. You have to realize that the pill won't take away your emotional issues that are causing your stress.

Getting some kind of therapy may be a great idea if you can't let go of the stress on your own. By speaking with a therapist, they can help you to sort things out and let go of the old stuff that is holding you back. Many people have had so much stuff from their past that they have never let go of. They are just letting it fester within them and holding that anger. Talking with a therapist can really help with long term issues. Some people think they don't need a therapist. They say "I'm not crazy, I don't need a shrink". You know we now live in a time of healing and that word shrink is just an old belief system. You don't have to be crazy to talk to a therapist, you would be crazy not to. Get the help if you need it!

Holistic Healing comes in many forms that you will read about in this book. Many modalities my sister and I do at our center. Below I will list some healing modalities and some you will read about in this book. Others that we don't do feel free to research them on the internet or check out some books about the different subjects.

- Therapeutic Massage*
- Reflexology*
- Ear Candling*
- Reiki*
- Theta Healing*
- Hypnosis*
- Meditation*
- Chakra Balancing*
- Crystal Healing*
- Clarity Breathwork*
- IET (Integrated Energy Therapy)*
- Traggar*
- Acupuncture
- Soul Connection and Healing*
- Psychotherapy
- Social Worker/Therapy
- Rolphing
- Holistic Nutritionist
- Shamanism

- Light Therapy
- Color Therapy
- Sound Therapy
- Angel Therapy*
- Spiritual Counseling*
- EFT (Emotional Freedom Technique)
- Holistic Doctors
- Qi Gong*
- Tai Chi
- Soul Coaching
- Yoga*
- Cupping
- Quantum Touch
- And so many more

Anything with a * next to it represents a modality that is done at our center.

Depending on your issues and illness you may have depends on what you need for a therapy. Whatever you decide is fine, just be sure you get what you need to lead your mind, body and soul onto a path of health and healing.

**This is in no way intended to replace traditional medicine in any way. Please seek medical attention when needed and use holistic therapy as a compliment to your medical care. Only you know what is right for you.

Affirmation: Today I choose to be happy and healthy.
I always look and find ways to stay healthy. I now release what no longer serves me so that I can now move forward in complete health.

I—INTUITION

Intuition is the ability to know information through senses other than our five natural senses. We are all born with intuition and use it all the time. Many just don't realize they are using it. They chalk it up to a coincidence or just a feeling. Well there are no coincidences and that feeling is intuition. Many people believe that you have to be psychic, a card reader or a medium to be intuitive. You don't. The only difference between you and a psychic is that a psychic is open to it, trust the information they get and more in tune to the information they receive. You can do this too if you just do a few things. First begin to meditate (Clear the mind), learn to connect with the guidance, trust what you get and believe that you can do it.

Think back to a time when you got a gut feeling. Did you follow through with that feeling or did you ignore it? Having a gut feeling is being intuitive. It is called clairsentience (discussed in Divine Guidance Chapter). It also has been referred to as "I had a feeling that was going to happen". Either way you are receiving intuitive guidance. Ever think about someone and the phone rings. Guess who? It's them. This is

Claircognizant, having a knowing. How many times have you seen a sign that make you go huh? The universe knows how to place things in our path so we see them. Maybe this sign has something to do with something you are going through or decision your trying to make. These signs can repeat themselves until you get it. Know that if you see a sign three times it is a definite sign . . . go with it.

I do many Angel card readings where the Angels, guides and/or loved ones from the other side come through and tell me that they are talking to the person I am reading for. When I relay the message, the client tells me that they don't hear anything. I ask them, have you ever had a conversation with yourself in your head? They usually say yes. I then explain to them that they are talking to their Angels, Guides and/or loved one's. This is a way that they talk to us. You have to understand that when you ask a question in your head and then answer it, that answer had to come from somewhere. This is clairaudience.

So as you can see we are all intuitive. We are all born with this gift. Some just tend to lose it as they grow up. Some of the reasons intuition is lost is due to our up bringing, religion, society, teachers, puberty, peer pressure and skeptics. We never fully lose our intuition though. We still have gut feelings or have those moments when we think, something told me that would happen or those aha moments. Ever just sit and watch children? They tell us stories of talking to Grandma or uncle Joe. We know they have passed on years before, but the children can describe them, see and talk to them. Babies are the best. Fresh into our world and still fully connected to the other side. They can see everything. I remember feeding my son as a baby and he would just stare at the space to the side of the chair and then give a little smile. I knew that my family was there watching and looking over him. Imaginary friends are another way that children connect. They are playing with someone, we as adults are the only ones who say imaginary. Many don't believe in spirit and the other side.

As a child, I had a friend. My mother would say that I had an imaginary friend, but today I know better. She has followed me throughout life and today she comes with me to my office and back home after. Her name is Amelia. One of my twins who is very intuitive see's her in our home. She will tell me "Mom that girls is here again and running around the kitchen". In fact there are times when Amelia will leave residue on my glass sliding door. It will be the size of a quarter or smaller and at the height a child would be. I know it's her because just like any other kid, I no sooner wash the glass doors and there is a spot on the door again . . . and I'm the only one home.

I remember as a child around the age of seven. Whenever I was alone, I could hear people talking to me constantly and could see their faces all around me. Now I didn't understand at that time what was going on, so one day I asked my Mother what it meant when people heard voices in their head. She replied, "That means they are crazy". Well you know I shut that thing off as soon as I heard that. My mother did not want me to be like her, psychic. I know she knew what I was talking about. That's all it took to shut it off, total refusal to acknowledge it anymore.

Today in my home we are very open about intuitiveness, God, Angels and Guides. My children know that if they get something intuitive they can come to me and ask me about it. They know that no one at home thinks that they are crazy. I don't want them to lose that gift. Today it is best to be open about spirituality and such. We need that intuitive guidance. We need to stay open to it. Today it also more accepted than it was back in 1975. Back then they would commit you for hearing voices. Of course you will always have skeptics but we can feel more comfortable about being psychic or intuitive.

So how do you re-open your intuitive side? First know that you can do it, believe it! Then it is practice, practice, and practice. Meditation is key. You need that quiet time for yourself and for the ability to connect. Pay attention to signs, messages and thoughts that just pop into your head from nowhere. Trust what you are feeling, seeing, hearing or sensing. It would be nice if it was as easy as flipping an on switch but it is not. Look at how many years you have been closed to it. It will take time. I have been doing my holistic work five and half years now and it took me sometime to get where I am today. The more you work at it, the faster it will come. Stay positive and don't give up.

People tell me all the time that they are too busy to sit still and meditate. I tell them even if you start with five minutes a day, it's a start. If they can find time in their busy lives to fit in more work, then they should be able to fit in five minutes for themselves. I think the best time is right as you wake up when your mind is clear or at the end of the day right before you lay down in bed. Stay sitting up for those five minutes and take three deep breaths and just let everything from your busy day just leave your body and mind. Then just sit quietly. If a thought comes in, acknowledge it, let it go and go back to quiet. Even if you have a break at work, take a few minutes to just be and let yourself recharge. You don't have to worry about whether you are doing it right, chanting an OM or sitting in a lotus position. All you need to do is sit comfortably, feet on the floor, close your eyes, take three deep breaths (in through the nose and out the mouth) and just clear your mind. Again if stuff pops in, acknowledge it then let it go. Here is a meditation that you can use to connect with your guides, angels or loved ones.

Visualize yourself in a beautiful garden. See it as you want. See the trees, flowers, shrubs, the sky, the colors and anything else you want there. Now see yourself placing two chairs in your garden. You sit in one and call in your guide, angel or loved one ro sit in the other. Just watch to see who comes to you. Don't worry if you don't see who it is. Pay attention to sensing or feeling someone there with you. If you don't know who they are, then ask. Then ask if they have a message for you. If you have any questions ask them for guidance. Be patient when waiting for answers. You may get it right away you may not. Be sure to go with whatever pops in your head first. The first thing is the right thing. Take your time and sit as long as you need. When you are finished, bring yourself back, take a deep breath and open your eyes.

You can do this meditation for five minutes or thirty. It's up to you. I would have you start small and work your way up. This garden is your sacred space where you can go anytime to just be or to receive guidance.

Daydreaming is another form of meditation. Did you ever come out of a daydream and feel relaxed or got an answer to a question you have had on your mind? Daydreaming is so wonderful, you feel like the rest of the world has just disappeared. This is a great way to clear your mind and just focus on what comes to you. Remember as a child you would daydream. You may have seen things that were amazing; premonitions of what you would be when you grew up or just feel like you weren't here anymore. Only to have your bubble busted when someone yells, "Stop daydreaming". If I knew then what I know now, I would have never let go of that childlike innocence and state of intuitiveness.

Affirmation: I am open to receiving guidance from spirit.
I easily get to my meditative state. I have more than enough time to meditate.

I—INTENTION

Intention is everything when you are doing healing work. It is also important when you are setting out to do something. I'm sure you have heard the saying, "They had such good/bad intentions". Well this is true. You decide what intentions you are going to put out there. Are you trying to do good or are you trying to bring ill will to someone.

During my healing work I set out my intentions that the person I am working on receive the healing energy that I am passing on to them and that they feel the effects of it. When I do Reiki distance healings, it is the same. It is all done with intention. I close my eyes and see the energy going to that person and healing what ever needs to be healed.

Intentions can be very strong and powerful. I remember getting a call from someone I know and she told me she had a bad cold and asked if I would send her some healing. So of course I said yes and would do it when I got off the phone. We hung up and I had a client walk in to talk for a moment, so I didn't do the healing right then, but had set my intentions that I was sending healing to the person that I just got off the phone with. Well ten minutes later the phone rang and it was that woman. She said thank you for the healing I feel so much better. She continued to tell me that right after we got off the phone she could feel tingling in her forehead, felt a pop and everything started to drain from her sinus and nasal passages. I then told her that I hadn't even sent it yet. I had set my intentions to send it, but I hadn't actually done the Reiki part yet. I did do the Reiki part right after we got off the phone so she could continue to get healing through out the day.

So you see intention is everything and when you have been doing healing for a while like me, sometimes all you have o do is think about sending healing and it starts before you do. The longer you have been doing healing work the more powerful the intentions can be.

Prayer is another form of intention. I'm sure you have prayed for someone at some point. Well when you pray for someone you are setting your intentions that this person receive help and/or healing. Then you have times when there are multiple people praying for the same person. Now that intention is multiplied for help and healing.

Many times I will get a call or e-mail from someone asking for healing for a loved one who is very ill. So I do, but then I also sent out a e-mail to my people asking that prayers and healing be sent to that person. Well now the responses come back, sure thing, will do, sending healing now and so on. The intention of a mass healing is amazing. The power of prayer!

When my father was diagnosed with a bleeding aneurysm in his brain I was so worried for him. I sent out a e-mail to my whole contact list asking for prayers and healing, that he would make it through the surgery and recover completely. I received e-mail after e-mail of prayers, healings and good intentions that he would be well again. I was amazed and printed out every single on for my Dad. He was blown away by the out pouring support. He even started to tear up. He was so grateful. He did make it through the eight-hour surgery and recovered fully.

Setting intentions is on the same idea as manifesting. You put the thought out there of what you want, believe it to be true and wait for it to happen. Intention is the strong thought of what of want and manifesting is the process of making it happen. They work together. When you manifest you need to follow your thoughts, guidance and so on. How it is going to happen is not the important part, but following that guidance to get your end result is. Be sure to follow that guidance.

When I knew that I wanted to open a healing center with my sister, I put my intentions out there to find a place that would be perfect for us. I wanted it all set up for us, treatment rooms, waiting area, reception area with a desk and in a good location. I didn't want to have to do any construction, I wanted to be able to pretty much move right in. I stayed positive and followed the guidance of my guides and angels. Well it worked, one day while driving down a street that I drive down almost daily, it was like someone took my steering wheel and turned it into this parking lot. Now I had seen a sign saying space available, but looking at the building you couldn't tell where it was. So I said to my angels "OK I will go in and ask". I did and to my surprise there was space and it was down these stairs not visible to the outside front of the building. Whenever she opened the door at the bottom, I was amazed. This space had everything I set out to manifest. It even had it's own private entrance and parking right in the back of the building. All we had to do was paint and move in . . . perfect! We were so grateful for this wonderful space and now have been here over five and a half years.

After we opened I remember putting more intentions out there of what else we wanted for our center. I had said I want to increase what we do here. I want people who teach yoga, classes, do more types of healing work and sell things that pertain to our work, like crystals, oils, CD's, books and so on. Well in less than a year we found that there was another large room opposite our space that was empty. We asked the landlord if we could use it and she said yes. So there is our yoga/class room. Then right after that we started putting a few things in our waiting area to sell and today we have hundreds of items in our little boutique. My sister and I also do more healing modalities than we did in the beginning and we have many practitioners that use our space to do their work as well. So when you decide that you want something, set your intentions, follow your guidance and manifest it . . . we did and it works!

Now as wonderful as intention is we have to discuss the bad intentions too. Many of us get angry at times with someone or something and say something we really don't mean. Well that is putting out your intention. When you set your intention in this state of anger/sadness you will get what you asked for, although it may not be what you really mean or want. For example: You get into an argument with someone you love and in the moment of anger you say or think, I wish I were alone. This is an intention even if you don't mean it. Remember be careful for what you ask for . . . wish granted.

So now the first thing you want to do is say "cancel, cancel, cancel" Then say something positive like "I love this person and we get along in harmony". By doing that it lets the universe know that you didn't mean it and only want good to come out of it. Now we all have thing called the ego and it loves to jump in front and take over. The ego is negative and you need to push it aside and bring through the heart center even in the bad times. Thought are things, they really are. So please be careful of your thoughts. Even if you do not speak your intentions the universe can still hear them and they can manifest.

When you want to place your intentions out there to the universe, God, angels or whom ever. Say or think of what you want, be specific and always ask for it for your highest and best, the highest and best of all involved, better than you could ever imagine. Now let it go and know and trust that it is coming to you. Be patient because you will get it when the time is right. You will know when it is time because you will get that pull and urgency that the time has come. Follow your signs, messages and guidance from the universe and you will be a master of manifesting.

Affirmations: I am now attracting what I need and want.

I am letting go of what no longer serves me and only live in the positive.

J—JOURNALING

Journaling is something we all should be doing. Remember as a child or teen you had or most had a diary. Well having a journal is the same. The only difference is what we write in it now. As a child I would write down my dreams, desires, my good days, my bad and so on. I grew up and thought diaries are only for kids. Well since I have been doing my spiritual work I have been writing in my journal. What a God send. My journal can be like my best friend. I write in it all the time. I write my goals, dreams, positive affirmations, what I am grateful for, my good news and my bad news. This is my way of sharing everything with God.

I tell my clients that they should have one and USE IT! Many tell me they have one but don't use it. Journaling is a great way of releasing what is bothering you. Sometimes we don't have anyone to talk to or what we need to talk about we would never tell anyone close to us. If you write it in your journal it is a way of letting it go and the only one listening is God and he/she is willing to listen to anything you have to say without judgment.

I have been journaling now for five years and the journals are piling up. I do like to go back and re-read them every once in a while to see what has changed in my life, what I have let go of and what goals I have achieved. It is amazing. You should journal everyday even if it is only a few lines to say how your day was. I also use my angel cards daily. I draw one card for a daily message and write it down in my journal. You can see the pattern of the messages when you keep track of them.

Journaling can be very meditative too. I have had times when I think to myself, what am I going to write and then a thought comes in and I start to write. Well before you know it I have written five or more pages and all I did was write what I was hearing in my head, the feelings I was having and it just keeps going from there. When you are quiet and journaling it is a great time to get messages from spirit. I know many times I would be conflicted about something and just sitting there writing about it, I would start getting answers and messages helping me to figure it out. Journaling helps to give you clarity, because your focus is only on the pen, journal and your thoughts.

Dreams are another thing you should write down in your journal. Many people tell me that their dreams are very vivid and clear but they just don't understand what they mean. I am not a dream interpreter but I know enough that you need to journal about them even if it is only bits and pieces. Dreams are a way fro the angels, guides and loved ones to talk to us. Leave a journal by your bedside, so that when you wake up you can write down everything you remember while it is still fresh. Otherwise you start to forget your dreams or only remember half of it.

Dreams can be messages from the divine or it can be a visit from a loved one. Ever have a dream of someone who has passed and in the dream you talk, hug and it is so real, so vivid. Well that was a visit not a dream. Messages can be given in dreams. You may only get a little at a time or you can get a full prophecy of things to come. Be sure no matter how much you get, write it all down and if it doesn't make sense to you now, it will later when you get more information.

You can't always take dreams literal either. I have people come see me and are freaking out because they saw something bad in a dream and think that it is going to come true. Not always the case. You have to look at what sticks out most in the dream and them look at the context of it. What is referring to? For example if you see someone get killed, it doesn't mean they will be. Instead look at it like this, what part of that person do you not like and you don't want to be like. Is that the part you would like to see gone in you and that person? You see dreams use a lot of symbolism. You have to pick apart the pieces and then you will understand what they mean.

If you are someone who has trouble remembering your dreams then ask the angels for help. Dear Angels, please help me to have clear and vivid dreams and that I will have full recollection of in the morning. The most important thing to remember is to leave the journal by your bed and as soon as you wake up, start writing. Even if it is during the night, because if you go right back to sleep you may not remember when you wake in the morning. It is best to write it down while it is fresh in your mind.

Things to write in your journal:
Dreams
Desires
Goals
Releasing negativity
Positive affirmations
Messages from the divine
Gratitude
Anything else you feel you need to express

Affirmation: I express myself daily in my journal. I have plenty of time for journaling.

I now release my negativity in my journal and move forward.

J—JUDGMENT

Judgment is basing an opinion as fact without knowing the facts and accepting it as truth. Many tend to judge others quickly without knowing the person or their circumstances. I call this gossip, another word for judgment. We have all done it from time to time. Some have learned to let that go and come from a place of love while others stay stuck in the drama and judgment. We all need to come from a place of compassion instead of judgment.

I have learned over time how bad judgment can be. I have let it go and when I see someone who is struggling, I don't judge. Instead I think to myself that the person must be going through a tough time and that's why they act the way they do. I feel compassion for them and send them prayers. As the old saying goes, unless you walk in a persons shoes, you don't know what their life is like.

Judgment can also be a form of jealousy. How many times have you or someone you know expressed feelings like, "look at her, she has so much, I wonder what she did to get it, she doesn't deserve it, why don't I have it"? Well maybe that person is living a life of harmony and balance. You haven't found yourself yet, maybe that's why you don't have all those things she does. Don't judge someone else for something you don't have yet.

Divorce I believe is one of the biggest judgment situations. Many will dwell on judging the other person. Right away we pick sides and rush to judge who is at fault. Now don't get me wrong, I believe there are times when people should divorce. The situations I want to bring up is when people do pick sides and just listen to one spouse or the other and believes everything that one person has to say without hearing the other side of the story. Same situation here, unless you live with the person(s) you don't know what goes on behind closed doors. There could be abuse, alcoholism, drugs, cheating or any other reason. You still have no right to judge. There are reasons for these behaviors, not that they are right but there is a reason.

So unless you know what this person went through in their life to make them the way they are . . . drop the judgment. All I know is that anyone going through a divorce needs compassion, love and someone to be there for him or her.

We are so quick to judge others. When the only person we should be judging is ourselves. Only we know our truths. Then when we realize our truths we can fix or change what needs to be changed. Even God does not judge us. We were taught to believe that God does, but how can they teach that God is all loving and on the other hand say that God is judgmental. Being judgmental is a negative emotion and God does not hold any negative emotions. Judgment is an ego-based emotion and God does not have an ego. No matter what we do in life God only loves us.

I do believe that we are the only ones who will judge ourselves once we go to the other side. We will go over our life time and see what we did right and what we did wrong. We will see what we learned and what we didn't. Then we let it go and if there is more for us to learn to higher our souls we will come back to live out another life. So I think I am going to do everything I can to learn now, because I don't think I want to come back again. I think we have the toughest job, to make it through this life here on earth. I once read that if a soul can make it here they can make it anywhere. So learn your lessons now, only go with love and help others to do the same.

I have learned through many teachers and books that when we judge another it is because we recognize that trait within ourselves. Let's say you judge "Sue" because you can see that she is lacking in self-confidence and won't move forward with what it is she wants to do. Well you recognize this because you are lacking in self-confidence yourself somewhere in your life. Maybe you see that "Peter" is angry and you think to yourself, that Peter is always angry, what is his problem? Well look at your life. What is it you are angry at or who are you angry at? It is probably not for the same reason, but you are recognizing the anger.

Now you're probably thinking just because someone is angry, it doesn't mean you are. Well it does if you are doing it with judgment. You see you can look at someone and see that they are angry and be compassionate, meaning you know the emotion they are dealing with, but if you judge then it is because you recognize that emotion within yourself. Pay attention to anytime in the past that you have judged someone and see where in your life you were feeling that same emotion that you were judging. Then do what you can to change that part of yourself.

Always work at releasing judgment when or if you find yourself judging someone. Stop and think I will not judge instead I will send this person love and compassion. I have learned to do this. It was not easy, but I have done it. I think we are programed to think we are supposed to judge and pass gossip. I no longer do this. I first think to myself, there is a reason why this person acts the way they do. I do not dwell in the drama. If I want drama I will watch a good television show. When I hear others judging someone, I say the same to them, maybe there is a reason they are acting that way. Maybe there is something going on in their life that is not well.

You cannot excel on your soul level if you're going to live in the negative. Stay positive, release judgment, be compassionate and show everyone love. Your soul will thank you for it.

Affirmations: I now release judgment about myself and others.
I now live with a compassionate heart and send love out to all.

K—KINDNESS

Kindness is an act that we should be showing and practicing everyday with everyone. We spend so much time running around with blinders on and don't pay attention to those around us who may need our help. There are those who expect everyone to help them, but won't lift a finger to help anyone else. People take things for granted and just think everything will be handed to them or they are not going to help anyone because no one helps them. Well it has to start somewhere. You can be the big person and offer to help. As they say it's a two way street. Do something nice and kind for someone and it will be returned to you. Someone will do something nice for you. This is all part of giving and receiving.

Kindness is a simple act. It can be as simple as holding a door open for someone, saying hello to a stranger, picking up something someone dropped, allowing a car to pass before you, offering a helping hand, be that ear to listen to a friend, that shoulder to cry on. Whatever it is practice kindness. If we all did this, the world could and would be a better place. We all need to slow down a little and really pay attention to the little things.

Before I opened my healing center and had children, I worked as a CAN in a nursing home. It would drive absolutely crazy when certain co-workers would refuse to do certain task because, "It wasn't their job". Give me a break. When I saw that something needed to be done, I just did it. If someone needed a hand, I was there to help. When we would work as team, everything always went much smoother and everyone was happier. If we all had that same attitude of "it's not my job" nothing would get done. Shoe acts of kindness and work together. If you can't get everyone to do this, then work with the ones who will.

Showing acts of kindness is another way to show love. When you are kind too, your heart shines and isn't that we are all working towards? I truly believe that today more and more people are looking to bring more happiness and love into their lives. I see it with my clients, returning and new clients. They come to learn how to be more positive, let go of the old and move forward. They all want the same thing, a life with peace, harmony and love.

When you find that someone is being mean or hurtful, send them love anyway. Remember not to judge. You don't know what is going on in their life. The more of us who practice love and kindness, the more we are putting positive energy out into the world. We need that more than ever right now. Our world has gotten so much busier, more stressful and more negative. It is time to change this! Together we can do this. So please practice kindness and send your love and kindness out to everyone and everything in this wonderful world of ours.

Kindness is something we have to show ourselves as well. More times than not we are right there to show kindness someone else but when it comes to ourselves we can be very negative. We put ourselves down; we don't give ourselves credit for being a perfect part of God and hi/her world. How many times have you heard someone say or said about yourself, I'm fat, I'm ugly, I'm not good enough, I'm not smart enough and so on. Please people give yourself some credit. You are a wonderful person and you need to express that same love and kindness to yourself.

It all starts with you. When you can express this kindness to yourself you will be able to express it openly to others too. Some find it hard to do this for others when they can't even do it for themselves. Start with you and tell yourself everyday what a great person you are and before you know it you will be on your way to a better you.

Affirmations: I now choose to be kind to myself. I am special. I show kindness to others and to the world, so we live in peace.

K–KARMA

Karma is the act of putting out good or bad and getting the same back in his life or in the next one. I'm sure you have heard the saying "What goes around, comes around". This is so true. When you put out positive, you will get positive back. When you put out negative know for sure that will come back to you too. This is what they call cause and effect.

When someone is always negative and does and says things from the ego, notice how bad things follow them. Let's say you say something bad about someone, then something bad will be said about you. If you were to steal from someone, something will be stolen from you. If you were to put out bad intentions to someone, know it will come back to you in one form or another.

Here is an example: Let's say "Paul" decides he is going to open a store that sells gifts. Then a few months later this woman "Sarah" decides to open a store a few blocks away as well. She is selling gifts too. "Paul" gets angry and competitive and says "I'm better than she is, she will never make it". Then he proceeds to tell people that her store is terrible, over priced and she doesn't know what she is doing.

Now "Sarah" works from her heart, always tries to do her best to get her customers what they want and always smiles. Now who do you think made it with a successful business? "Sarah" did great and today is thriving with a huge customer flow. "Paul" went under within a year because he worked from negativity and the ego. He got back what he put out and "Sarah" did too . . . positive return!

Karma doesn't always pertain to the negative. Karma is for the positive as well. In these past few years as a spiritual person and teacher, I have had wonderful karmic experiences. I do a lot for others, I always do my best to help those who seek it and strive to keep learning so I can pass it on. I have gotten so much back in so many different ways. It is amazing.

The intentions that my sister and I out when we opened our healing center was to bring health, happiness, freedom, peace, tranquility and love to everyone who entered. We treat our place like home. We treat everyone like family. We don't run our place like a corporate business. We treat it with love and positive intention. It has come back to us ten fold. I know people who have tried to do the same kind of business as ours and failed, due to the fact all they looked at was the money and how much they could make. Nothing mattered except for how many people they could get through the door and how much they would make. Not the way to run a healing center. I believe that you need to have a heart as big as God's to want to help people like we do.

I have given discounts and free services to some that I know need the healing but don't have the money. I get rewarded with gifts sometimes and then there are times all they can give is a simple thank you and a hug, which is fine with me. My job is to help people heal no matter what they can do for me. I know if I do my part, God will do his. He/she put my sister and me together in this center for a reason. I also do free Reiki treatments for cancer patients here at the center as well as at a local hospital. My sister does chair massage at a local breast care center when they hold ladies events. I thank all who have given to my sister and I. Without all of you, we would not be here.

Karma can be received now or in the next life. Before I really knew what karma was, I would question about those who break the law. Let's say a murderer. There is a man who goes crazy shooting everyone in his work place and then in a stand off with the police, they shoot and kill the gunman. Well where is his karma, he is dead? Well today I understand so much more. He did die for what he did, but he will also have to come back and live another life to learn all over again. He will have to fulfill his karmic debt and learn for his souls purpose.

Karma can happen right away, it can take years or even happen in the next life. Either way know and trust that it will happen. I believe we all have karma to a certain extent. We may be in this life now to learn and clear karma from our past life. Think about what you maybe struggling with in this life, that maybe a lesson you need to learn. You can find out what your past life was by doing past life regression or see someone who does past life readings.

Maybe in your past life you were someone who made fun of someone who was blind. You may just come into this life as a blind person or become blind in this life so that you can experience what that person in your past life had to experience and feel. You may have had a past life that you were an abuser. This life you may be the one who getting abused. See how that karmic debt can follow you. So please always do your best to live in the positive, from the heart and not in the ego. Your ego will get you in trouble. Know that what ever you put out; be prepared to get it back, good or bad.

Affirmation: I always treat others, as I want to be treated.
                      I send out love so that I can receive love.

L—LETTING GO

Letting go can be something that is very difficult for some people. Many have been hurt by others, hold onto guilt of what they have done, hold onto loved ones that have passed, hold onto the past or don't forgive.

Holding onto old "stuff" will result in you not moving forward, not living in peace, love, joy and happiness. Ever feel like your body is heavy, sluggish, no energy or a heavy tight feeling in our chest? Well that means your holding on to old "stuff" and haven't let it go.

What is "OLD STUFF"? Being hurt by someone. We have all been there at one time or another. Either by a relationship, family, friends, co-workers and so on. People will make us angry at times but what we do is hold onto that anger. It is all right to get angry, we are human, but you need to forgive and let it go in a reasonable amount of time.

GUILT: I wrote about this earlier in the book. We all have guilt at times. Maybe we feel we didn't do enough, did something or said something wrong, didn't raise our children right, didn't put enough into our relationship and it goes on. If you did not do any of these things intentionally, then you need to let it go. If you did, then forgive yourself, fix it and move on.

Holding onto loved ones that have passed: we are always saddened when we lose a loved one and we take time to grieve. I have met people who have held onto the grief for years and are still holding on. You cannot do this. This is living in the past and moving forward with your life.

This happens when there are unresolved issues that were not fixed when a person passes, they didn't get to say goodbye, the death was tragic or there was such a bond between the two people, that one cannot live without the other. We are all meant to live on this earth for a certain amount of time and it is our time, it is our time. We can't change that. We all lose loved ones. My sister and I lost our Mother to cancer in 2006, but I knew that she was still with us and always will be. We knew we still had to move forward and live our lives. We have our own purpose to fill before our day comes. We do miss her very much still, but we both know that we can talk to her anytime and get signs from her, which we do.

Do whatever you need to, to let go and move forward. I don't mean forget these people. I mean find ways to make peace with it and live your life. You can always talk to those who have passed anytime you want. They can hear you. You can also seek out help with your feelings that you are having trouble letting go of. You can do Reiki, Theta, Breathwork, counseling, therapy or even see a spirit medium (psychics that can communicate with the other side) or what ever will work for you to move on. Let go of the grief and hold onto the love.

Holding onto the past: What happened in the past is the past. You cannot change it or worry about it. When you worry about the past all you are doing is wasting energy on something you can't change. Instead use that energy to move forward. You need to forgive whatever happened in the past whether it is about someone, something or yourself. Let it go and move on.

Many times we are holding on to "stuff" we think we have to let go of and sometime this "stuff" in buried deep in our subconscious. We may believe in our conscious minds that we are over what ever it is, when in all reality we are not. I learned this first hand. I had issues with my mother when I was younger and after she passed I was sure I was over it. Well I was wrong. You see my mother was a drinker. I hated it so much. She is what they call a closet drinker. She would drink after we all went to bed. If we went out to eat she would have a glass or two of wine, good excuse to drink, we were out to dinner. As I got older into my teens I was stuck with making dinner because while we were at school she would drink and then would go sleep it off before Dad got home.

The older I got the worse it got. I tried getting her to stop, but she didn't think she had a problem. Then she would tell me to mind my own business and that I would not understand. I held this in and never told anyone about my mom. The only person who knew was my best friend Kim. I mean really, as a teen how embarrassing to bring a friend home and your mom is toasted.

When my mom passed away, I thought that was it. I really thought now that she is gone all my stuff went with her . . . wrong. I still had it in me. I never told her how I felt. It doesn't go with her; I'm the one who had to let it go. I just didn't know that yet.

I attended a spiritual retreat in 2009 with my sister and some friends. That's when I was introduced to Breathwork. Well that is what I needed. During my breathwork, I got to tell my mother exactly what I wanted after all this time. I really gave it to her. I really needed to do this and when it was over I felt 1000 lbs. lighter. I had finally let it go. I let go of all that stuff that was holding me down and today I have a really good connection with her. Don't get me wrong, during my younger years, I loved my mother dearly, I just didn't love what she was doing. It felt so good now that I had let that go and getting the ability to openly discuss it without the embarrassment and guilt. A true breakthrough for me.

Look over your life now and in the past and see if there is something or a situation that you are still holding onto. Do what ever you can to let it go. Try one of the modalities I mentioned earlier. Just know that one session is just the beginning of letting go. You will more than likely need a few sessions. Remember there could be years of build up and that will take time to break down and let go. Be patient with yourself and just keep working at it. Let Go and Let God!

Affirmation: I now release (name person or situation) so that I can live my life with a clear mind.
I am now releasing what no longer serves me, so I can move forward.

Try this simple meditation to help you release your "stuff"

Dear Archangel Michael, I ask you to please help me to let go of my fears, doubts and what no longer serves me, so that I may move forward with love and light. Please use your spiritual vacuum to suck away any and all negative energy or lower energy from my mind, body and soul. Thank you Archangel Michael.

M—MASSAGE

Massage is a therapeutic service that is not considered a luxury any more but a necessity for some and a great way of relieving muscle pain and tension without the use of medications. This is another service we offer at our center. My sister Dora is the massage therapist. She is so good at what she does. I don't say this just because she is my sister, but because of all the compliments and feedback we get from clients. Massage is truly Dora's gift and she loves what she does, know that it is so beneficial to everyone.

There are many different types of therapeutic massage. I am going to write about the types we provide at Sisters of Solace.

*Swedish Massage—Massage is the manipulation of superficial layers of muscle and connective tissue to enhance the function and promote relaxation and well-being.

Massage involves acting on and manipulating the body with pressure— structured, unstructured, stationary, or moving—tension, motion, or vibration, done manually or with mechanical aids. Target tissues may include muscles, tendons, ligaments, skin, joints, or other connective tissue, as well as lymphatic vessels, or organs of the gastrointestinal system. Massage can be applied with the hands, fingers, elbows, knees, forearm, and feet. There are over eighty different recognized massage modalities. The most cited reasons for introducing massage as therapy have been client demand and perceived clinical effectiveness. In professional settings massage involves the client being treated while lying on a massage table, or sitting in a massage chair. The massage subject may be fully or partly unclothed. Parts of the body may be covered with towels or sheets.

*Deep Tissue Massage—is the same as the above with the exception being the amount of pressure used. The more pressure the more the muscles are manipulated. A deep tissue massage is designed to relieve severe tension in the muscle and the connective tissue or fascia. This type of massage focuses on the muscles located below the surface of the top muscles. Deep tissue massage is often recommended for individuals who experience consistent pain, are involved in heavy physical activity (such as athletes), and patients who have sustained physical injury. It is not uncommon for receivers of deep tissue massage to have their pain replaced with a new muscle ache for a day or two. Deep tissue work varies greatly.

*Pregnancy Massage—Pregnancy massage has been found to reduce stress, decrease swelling in the arms and legs, and relieve aches and pains in muscles and joints.

It's a popular complementary therapy during pregnancy for back pain, when choices for pain relief, such as medication, are often limited. Not only can massage be physically beneficial, but the human touch can be comforting and provide emotional support during pregnancy. It has also been found to reduce anxiety and depression.

*Hot Stone Massage—involves the application of water heated stones of various sizes to key points of the body, giving a deep massage and creating sensations of comfort and warmth. The direct heat relaxes muscles, allowing manipulation of a greater intensity than with regular massage.

*Aromatherapy Massage—When you inhale essential oil molecules, messages are transmitted to the limbic system and affect heart rate, stress level, blood pressure, breathing, memory, digestion, and the immune system. Essential oils are also believed to be absorbed through the skin. Each essential oil has different healing properties. For example, some calm while others energize. Here are examples of the Aromatherapy Massages done at sisters . . .

Indulgent Chocolate Soothing Massage: A delicious, milk chocolate. Top notes of fruity butter and nuances of jasmine. Mid notes of chocolate, sweet honey, rose and coriander seed. With a creamy vanilla and powder at the base. Nourish your skin with a decadent Chocolate Massage Gel. Chocolate is full of anti-oxidants and Glycerides that delivers moisturizing lipids and fats that plump and firm the skin, your skin will thank you for it! This treatment leaves your skin soft, moist and radiant!

Tranquillite Massage: Everyone likes Lavender! It is a long-time soothing remedy and a delightful aroma. In harmony with other beneficial Essential Oils, this Lavender-based synergy provides a complete Aromatherapy experience that nurtures and calms the mind. It has a very fresh, yet relaxing aroma that makes it a great complement to any Therapeutic Massage. Contains: Essential Oils of Lavender, Lavendin Super, Orange, Geranium, Cedarwood, Wild Marjoram, Omanese Frankincense

Calming Aromatherapy Massage—Serene and sweet like a lake in full moonlight, this blend combines the "peace makers" among the Essential Oils, for a soothing and relaxing experience. The touch of Rose Oil added to this blend creates a blissful harmony with the Lavender.Contains: Essential Oils of Lavender, Orange, Geranium, Cedarwood, Marjoram, Omanese Frankincense, Rose.

Energizing Mint Therapeutic Massage—The power blend for times when you want to accelerate and excel! This blend is fresh and full of "minty" energy. It is also one of the bestselling blends, maybe because it is made with oils that also find use in the kitchen and smell simply delicious! Contains: Essential Oils of Spearmint, Peppermint, Rosemary, and a citrus twist of Orange, Red Grapefruit, Lemongrass.

Revitalizing Energy Massage—We have blended Citrus Essential Oils with Rosemary, Lemongrass and other energizing oils to evoke feelings of happiness, bliss and self-confidence. Contains: Essential Oils of Rosemary, Lemongrass, Orange, Ginger Root, Red Grapefruit, Mandarin Orange and Cinnamon Leaf.

Other forms of massage

Acupressure (a combination of "acupuncture" and "pressure") is a traditional Chinese medicine (TCM) technique derived from acupuncture. With acupressure physical pressure is applied to acupuncture points by the hand, elbow, or with various devices.

Anma is a traditional Japanese massage involving kneading and deep tissue work.

Ayurveda is a natural health care system originating in India that incorporates massage, yoga, meditation and herbal remedies. Ayurvedic massage, also known as Abhyangha is usually performed by one or two therapists using a heated blend of herbal oils based on the ayurvedic system of humors.

Bowen technique involves a rolling movement over fascia, muscles, ligaments, tendons and joints. It is said not to involve deep or prolonged contact with muscle tissues as in most kinds of massage, but claims to relieve muscle tensions and strains and to restore normal lymphatic flow. Because this technique is so gentle, so Bowen Therapy can be suitable for newborn baby to elderly. It is based on practices developed by Australian Tom Bowen and the practitioners are all over the world.

Lomilomi is the traditional massage of Hawaii. As an indigenous practice, it varies by island and by family. The word lomilomi also is used for massage in Samoa and East Futuna. In Samoa, it is also known as lolomi and milimili. In East Futuna, it is also called milimili, fakasolosolo, amoamo, lusilusi, kinikini, fai'ua. The Māori call it roromi and mirimiri. In Tonga massage is fotofota, tolotolo, and amoamo. In Tahiti it is rumirumi. On Nanumea in Tuvalu, massage is known as popo, pressure application is kukumi, and heat application is tutu. Massage has also been documented in Tikopia in the Solomon Islands, in Rarotonga and in Pukapuka in Western Samoa.

Medical Massage is a controversial term in the massage profession. Many use it to describe a specific technique. Others use it to describe a general category of massage and many methods such as deep tissue massage, myofascial release and triggerpoint therapy as well as reiki, osteopathic techniques, cranial-sacral techniques and many more can be used to work with various medical conditions. Massage used in the medical field includes decongestive therapy used for lymphedema which can be used in conjunction with the treatment of breast cancer. Light massage is also used in pain management and palliative care. Carotid sinus massage is used to diagnose carotid sinus.

Myofascial release refers to the manual massage technique for stretching the fascia and releasing bonds between fascia, integument, and muscles with the goal of eliminating pain, increasing range of motion and equilibrioception. Myofascial release usually involves applying shear compression or tension in various directions, or by skin rolling.

Thai massage—Known in Thailand as "ancient/traditional massage", Thai massage originated in India and is based on ayurveda and yoga. The technique combines massage with yoga-like positions during the course of the massage; the northern style emphasizes stretching while the southern style emphasizes acupressure.

Trigger point therapy—Sometimes confused with pressure point massage, this involves deactivating trigger points that may cause local pain or refer pain and other sensations, such as headaches, in other parts of the body. Manual pressure, vibration, injection, or other treatment is applied to these points to relieve myofascial pain. Trigger points were first discovered and mapped by Janet G. Travell (president Kennedy's physician) and David Simons. Trigger points have been photomicrographed and measured electrically and in 2007 a paper was presented showing images of Trigger Points using MRI. These points relate to dysfunction in the myoneural junction, also called neuromuscular junction (NMJ), in muscle, and therefore this modality is different from reflexology, acupressure and pressure point massage.

There are so many more types of massage and body work out there. To list them all would be too much, so I only added modalities that I have read about or have knowledge of. You can always look them up on the internet so you can see if any of them are right for you. The list I provided was taken from; http://en.wikipedia.org/wiki/Massage

Therapeutic massage is not just for the relief of muscle tension, but many have been known to have emotional release as well. There are many times when a client will just start crying or open up about what is going on with them. Massage therapist can be like your hairdresser, you can tell them anything. They always keep everything confidential. Where we are a healing center we always encourage people to let go of the old stuff, allow healing to happen and feel the healing taking place. Whether you come in for a massage or a reiki session, we help you to clear you mind, body and soul.

Massage is also a great way to let go of stress, tension and anxiety that we hold onto everyday due to work, others and just life in general. A massage will help you to feel completely stress free. As you are enjoying your massage you will feel the stress and tension just drain right out of you. You can always tell when you have too much stress, you feel the knots right in your shoulders, neck and upper back. So if you are feeling tight in these areas, it is time for a massage.

M—MEDITATION

Meditation is a form of quieting the mind, so you can relax and connect with God, Angels, Guides, the universe or your higher self. It is a way of letting go of the day, the stress and getting yourself back to center. Meditation has many benefits. Not only does it help you to clear your mind, but did you know that it can reduce blood pressure, reduce heart rate and relieve stress and tension.

Many people don't take enough time to just BE anymore. Everyone is constantly rushing around doing this and doing that. You really need to find time to quiet your mind even if you just take five minutes a day and work your way up from there. When you do this you are giving your mind a chance to rest and in time you will see that you will be less stressed and you will sleep better. So many people tell me they don't sleep well because their mind is constantly going. Always thinking of what they have to do the next day or they keep going over all the events of their day. When you meditate you are giving your mind a chance to let go of your day, relax and finally be quiet.

How do you meditate? First thing is not to give up trying. So many tell me that they give it up only after one or two times because they said their mind didn't get quiet. Meditation is a practice and you have to keep at it. Like anything else in life, you have to practice. It took me a while before I could sit still and clear my mind. On occasion I do find that I will drift off during meditation, but all I do is let that thought go and clear my mind again. After all I'm only human, just like all of you. Many things we will do in life will be a lifetime practice. It would be nice if we could just turn things on and that is it.

Remember as children we would get so determined to do something and we didn't give up. Why then as adults we try once or twice and that's it we give up and make excuses as to why we can't do it. We need to keep that same mind set as when we were kids. You have to have patience with yourself and give it time. The more you practice the easier it will get and you will be able to meditate. Meditating on a regular basis makes you a calmer person, more balanced and more positive.

Here is how to start. First you will want to find a quiet place where you will not be disturbed. If you want you can play some soft (instrumental) music in the back ground. Sit comfortably, close your eyes and take three deep breaths, in through the nose and out through the mouth. Breathing this way helps the body to relax faster. Then just continue to breathe normally and just focus on your breath. If you get thoughts in your mind and you probably will, just acknowledge it and then let it go. Then return to focusing on your breath. Do this for about five minutes. It may seem like forever, but in time you will breeze right through. Keep practicing and before you know it you will be able to meditate longer.

Now if you still find this way too difficult, and some do, then you might be better off with a guided mediation CD. With a guided meditation you have a person who guides you through every step. By listening to them that is your focus. They may have you visualize yourself on a beach somewhere, in a garden or some other peaceful place and then take you on a journey. At certain points they may leave you for a bit to enjoy the space you're in and then they will come back to continue guiding you. Again if you find your mind is wandering, just acknowledge it and let it go then go back to following the meditation. I recommend guided meditations to my clients who just have a real hard time with focus and they tell me that they found it easier to follow what someone was telling them rather than just sitting in complete silence and trying to stay that way. At some point you will be able to just sit and focus on your breath, but for now try the guided and just keep practicing.

At my center I hold monthly group meditations. I hold monthly group meditations. We have many who return month after month and we have new people too. The group is then led on a journey to where ever with whomever we call in. For example some of the meditations we do are Healing with the Angels, Manifesting with Archangel Michael, Blessed Mother meditation, Shape Shifting, Gratitude meditation, Chakra meditation, Shamanic Journey, Working with the For Elements and so many more. The energy in that room is amazing. Everyone has such a positive outlook and with the collective energy, we attract many Angels, Masters, Guides and loved ones who come and sit with us. Everyone has a great experience.

Don't worry if you are not a very visual person. This too can take time. As long as you listen and use your senses of feeling and knowing. You will do just fine. Many times people who are not visual tell me they are very relaxed after the meditation and could feel like their loved one was with them or they can sense that something is going on within them, like healing. Archangel Michael is one angel everyone can feel around them. I have to laugh to myself watching people meditate with Michael, because everyone is rubbing their nose or face like they have an itch. What this is, is Michael's wings. When his feathers touch people they feel it. Also people have told me that they felt Michael hugging them and he does do this, I feel it when he does. One woman I remember said she felt like his wings were wrapped around her hugging her tight, she felt so much love.

Other ways to meditate can be walking or daydreaming. Daydreaming puts you in a meditative state. It is like you left the room without really leaving the room at all. You forget all time when you do this. A person can receive guidance too when in this state, because you are in total focus of a clear mind. I have gotten ideas, messages and visions this way.

Walking is a great way to get out and meditate. Walking of course is healthy for you physically but mentally it is a great way to de-stress. When you go for a walk, count your steps 1-10 then back 10-1. This gives you a focus just like focusing on your breath. You can also just walk and let your mind sort out your thoughts or you can listen to meditation music or self-help CD's.

No matter which way you decide to meditate, be sure to do it every day. Start with as little as five minutes a day and work your way up to whatever amount of time is comfortable for you. Keep practicing and don't get discouraged. They say it takes 21 days to create a new habit so keep going, the benefits are amazing. You will feel better physically, mentally, emotionally and spiritually.

Affirmations: I meditate daily for my mind, body and soul.
   I always have time for myself to meditate daily.

M—MEDIUMSHIP

Mediumship is the ability to intuitively connect with those who have passed and are in spirit on the other side. People who do this type of work are called mediums. They help you to connect with your loved ones in spirit. Many seek out a medium because they need to hear and talk with their loved ones. Usually do to the fact that they miss them terribly, didn't have a chance to say goodbye, they have questions about how they died or they had unresolved issues with that person. Whichever the reason, you can get a lot of healing when you go to a medium.

As you now know, I do Angel card readings, Reiki and other healing work. Many times during my work I will get a loved one who comes through. The spirit(s) that come through will tell me who they are, describe what they look like and give me specific things about them, so this way the person I am working with will know who is coming through for them.

Mediums are not always psychics. They usually work with only spirit and do not give predictions. There are some who do, but mediums usually stick with connecting with spirit. If they do get something for your future it is because your loved one has told them. Mediums can bring healing to the person they are reading for through connecting with their loved one and confirming that life does go on, giving you the chance to say goodbye and helping you to fix whatever what was left undone. Our loved ones go to the place of love and light. Remember death is not the end, but the beginning of a new life on a different vibration.

We can all connect with the other side. As I said earlier, we are all intuitive. Think back to a time when you suddenly thought of a loved one who had passed. That is their way of letting you know that they are with you. Have you ever felt like something touched you? You look around and there is no one there. That's your loved one, they love to be around and let you know they are there. Sometimes it is just a light touch on the head, shoulder or face. Ever "think" you saw someone out of the corner of your eye? That is them as well. We can usually catch a glimpse of them in our peripheral vision. I tell my clients that if had the thought that you saw something/someone, then you did. You would have to see something for it to trigger the brain to say I saw something.

Loved ones love to leave us gifts. I'm sure you have heard of pennies from heaven. They like to leave coins around. The trick is to check the dates. You may find that the date is significant like a birthday, anniversary, a passing or just special event that happened in that year. They can also send us birds, butterflies, humming birds (a big one for me) and dragonflies. My sister in law called me a while back and told me of this robin that was sitting alone on a branch in the front yard. Now she new of the gifts from our loved ones because I had told her. So I told her to say Hi to the bird and ask it to come closer. Well not only did she do that but she also told the bird "Dad if that is you come to the branch near the window". To her surprise, the bird did. I love when these things happen.

I am sure many of you have dreamt of your loved one(s). Many people have told me that the dream was so vivid, like it was real. Well it was. When this happens, the dream is so vivid; it is a visit from your loved one(s). They always find ways of connecting with us. If they can't get to us when we are awake and busy, they will come in our dreams when our minds are not busy. You just have to work at being open to getting their messages, signs and other gifts. Don't pass things off as imagination or coincidence, because it isn't. Remember there are no coincidences.

Children and animals are very open to the other side. Children have clear minds and have not yet had them clouded with societies interpretation of what is right, wrong, acceptable or unacceptable. I have heard so many stories from people with children telling me that they have one child and when they play they hear them laughing and giggling as if they are playing with someone. The best on is when a small child tells their mom or dad that they were playing with grandpa, grandma or some other loved one that passed away before they were born. You know this has to be real, especially when the child give them specifics like their name, what they looked like and so on. Now there is no way of the child knowing this but yet they know.

Even babies will see spirit. I remember feeding my son his bottle and his eyes would be fixed on the corner of the room and then he would give a big smile. I know he saw my grandparents. Babies sometimes will be in their crib and you will see that they are staring at a certain area of the room and you're like wondering what they are staring at. They see loved ones. Those in spirit like to play with the babies too. I recall a time when my son was still in a crib and he had a stuffed frog that was called Tad. You could press the shapes and colors to learn. Well he was in his crib and I was downstairs with the baby monitor when I heard Tad start talking and it said "Hi". Well my son could not have done this because he was only four months old and Tad was on the other end of the crib. I know one of my grandparents or my husbands' dad was playing with him.

Animals are completely open to the other side. Watch your animals, they will stare at nothing, refuse to go into a room, bark at nothing and just seem strange. Over the years I have had many pets and can remember they all would have their moments of spirit sightings. I remember one cat I had would be running around playing as she rounded the corner to enter the next room, it was like she slammed on the brakes. She just had this look and stare. She would not go into this next room.

Animals are so open because unlike we humans, they do not have an ego they are pure unconditional love. They do have a personality but not an ego. If an animal is mean it is because someone made it that way. Animals can pick up on negative energy. So pay attention to your animals, they will let you know when your loved ones are around.

Speaking of animals I have a funny story. When one of my daughters was 7 years old she went to bed like usual and I think within ten minutes she was calling me. I asked what was wrong and she tells me she can't sleep, which was very unusual for her. I asked why and she tells me because there is a tiger that is staring at her from the foot of her bed. I start to laugh, not at her but at the fact that she just asked me the day before what her animal guide was. So I reminded her of this. She was so excited, said thank you and went to sleep.

Since then I encouraged her to start a journal with all the spirits she has talked to. Write down what she hears from them and so on. Well my daughter loves to draw so she started drawing the people she would see. My daughter can see and hear the spirits. I do encourage her and her brother and sister to be open to everything. In my house seeing spirit and talking with spirit is normal. We need to let the children connect with out having to worry if someone is going to think they are weird. I do tell my children not to talk about spirit and angels at school only because I don't need them to get picked on. I just tell them that school is a time for learning and that they can talk as much as they want once they get home.

There was a time after my mother passed away that my son was playing in the spare room at my Dads' house and he told me that he was playing with grandma. I told him that's great she likes playing with you. Next thing really confirmed to me that he did see her. He asked me why grandma was this high off the ground? He was referring to the fact that she was about three feet off the ground. Well the other side is only the next dimension from this one and spirits will appear three feet off the ground. If you or anyone you know had seen a spirit, you will notice that they seem to be floating across the floor. I have read in many books from different authors that the other side is right here three feet above this one and the only thing that separates us is the veil which happens to be thinning. Another belief I have is that at some point not far from now we will all be able to see spirit because of that thinning veil. We will see.

My other daughter is intuitive as well. She doesn't think so but she is. I have heard her many times talking to "No one". She would be talking, laughing and giggling while she was in bed. I would hear her in the middle of the nigh too. So as you can see, all three of my children are intuitive at some degree. There is nothing wrong with that. I rather be open about the other side and spirit so they keep their gift instead of losing it like I did at seven. I shut it off because I was told that I was crazy if I heard voices. It took me a long time to re-connect and get to the point I am at now. Support you children; don't make them feel like they are wrong or crazy.

So how do you connect with your loved ones, Practice! Meditating is a big part too. You have to have a clear mind and an open heart. Find a quiet place to sit without interruption. Sit comfortable, close your eyes, take a couple of deep breaths to relax and clear your mind. Ask Archangel Michael to surround and protect you. Now either out loud or in your head ask for a loved one to come through to you. Sit patiently and wait for something to come through. Pay attention to your thoughts, feelings, if you're sensing anything or seeing anything in your inner vision. Ask them to let you know that they are there. Listen for noises such as tapping, soft breath or any other noises that are not usual for where you are. If you feel like you didn't get anything, that's ok. It does take practice. Don't force anything. If you try to hard you can block it from happening. When you do connect with your loved one ask questions, wait for answers and just talk with them like you would when they were here. You can also ask them for a sign when they are around you. More likely than not they will give you a sign. Be sure to thank them when you are done.

I have connected with my mother this way. I asked her to come through to me and she did. I remember hearing "Hi honey" just the way she did when she was here. I had tears coming down my face the emotion was very strong. I continued talking with her for a while asking questions, getting responses, general conversation and then I thanked her. Until next time . . . I love you. So as you can see we are never truly alone. Our loved ones may have left the physical plane but are still here with us. All we need to do is be open to receive and trust they will be there when we ask.

Affirmations: I am open and ready to receive guidance from my loved ones. I am a channel that is always open to talk to my loved ones in spirit.

N—NEGATIVITY

Negativity is characterized by habitual skepticism and a disagreeable tendency to deny or oppose or resist suggestions or commands according to the dictionary. It is also what we call in the spiritual sense "The Ego". That little voice in your head that tears you down all the time. Tells you that you are not good enough, you don't have enough and so on.

I teach people how to turn their negativity around to a more positive outlook, love and light. Negative energy is very draining. It is wasted energy. Ever notice that when you are negative, you don't feel good and have lack of energy? When you are positive, smiling and having fun, you feel great and full of energy.

As the Law of Attraction says; If you put negative out there, you will get negative back. Put out positive and you will get positive back. This is truth! I have seen it and I live it . . . positive that is. See if any of these statements sound familiar to you or someone you know.

- *I always have bills.
- *I never have any money.
- *I never meet anyone new.
- *I should have _____. (this is living in the past)
- *Nothing ever goes right for me.
- *I can't _____.
- *I am always sick.
- *My car always breaks down.
- *It is always something. and so on . . .

All these statements are very negative. You have to turn these around to positive statements. Yes bad things do happen but you still need to turn it around into a positive. Even of it is not true yet, act as if it is. The more positive you put out there the more things will change for the better. Any time you catch yourself saying something negative, say cancel, cancel, cancel and then change it into a positive statement. So here are the positive statements to change those above.

*My bills are always paid on time.
*I have an abundant financial flow.
*I am attracting new people in my life who are perfect for me.
*I let go of the past and move forward with ease.
*All good things happen for me now.
*I can do anything I set out to do.
*I have a healthy energetic body.
*My car always works perfectly and gets me where I need to go.
*Everything works as it should and I am grateful.

Please understand you have to turn things around in your life in order for things to get better. Otherwise you will be stuck in that negative pattern. Be careful of what you think and say. Think of what you want your life to be. Do you want the negative, sadness and lack of energy or do you want happiness, joy, abundance and positive ness? I know I prefer the positive side of life, it feels so much better.

You will notice that when you use positive thoughts and words, everything falls into place. Your life will be better and everything will work in sync. It all starts with you. It takes practice and in time you will recognize right away when you're negative and change it instantly into a positive statement. Remember even if it is not true yet, say and think like it is and it will be. Then you just need to trust and believe. It can be hard at first but keep at it.

Another way to feel negativity is from other people. We are able to feel the negativity that others put out there. Their negativity hits you right in the solar plexus (chakra right above the belly button). For example, let's say you are introduced to someone new and when they approach you, you instantly get that gut feeling like there is something about this person you don't like and you feel like you want to take a step back away from them. You are feeling their negative energy. The same is true with positive people. When they are around you, you can feel their light and love.

When I am working at my center with clients, I always ground and protect myself because the people I am helping have issues they want worked on. These issues can be physical, emotional, mental or spiritual.

These energies are not the one's I want to feel. Then I have to disconnect from those people, meaning cut away from their energy and cleanse the room with sage (sage clears negative energy).

If you feel you are or know you are going to be in the presence of someone who is negative you need to call in Archangel Michael and ask him to surround you in his protective light and protect you from all negative energy and entities. Visualize this beautiful light all around you. Then send this person light and love, so that they may become more positive too. Negativity does not like positive or the dark does not like the light, so when you do this that person will either leave you alone or leave the room.

Here is another method to ward off negative energy from people. This is my favorite. Every time I tell someone to use this method they end up calling me the next day saying, Oh my gosh, you were right. That person just left the room and left me alone. Here it is. Visualize baby pink roses showering down all over that person who is negative and hold that vision for a minute. That's it. Easy huh? That is all it takes, just do that and you will be negative free. If you are in a situation that the person cannot leave the room (like work) then they will at least leave you alone. You see the little pink roses represent love and negative does not like it.

I realized this a couple of years ago when I was at a board meeting for a fundraiser. There was a woman there who didn't like me and she was very negative. I was sitting there with my friend and I started to shake. Just like when you have had too much caffeine. I couldn't believe it, even my friend was like "what is wrong"? I looked over and saw the reason. It was her. So I immediately visualized baby pink roses showering all over her. Before I knew the shaking stopped and within a few minutes she left the meeting saying "I have to go I can't stay here". Funny she never came to another meeting, I can't imagine why. Must have been those roses.

So if you live, work or have to be around anyone negative, remember the roses. Also you should make it a habit to surround and protect yourself with the white light or the beautiful light of Archangel Michael (Blue) before you even leave your house in the morning. This way you are already protected.

Negative energy in the home is not always an easy thing to live with. This can be from the person(s) you live with or it can be energy left behind from the past people who were there. If it a home or apartment that was occupied before and the people were negative or something bad happened there, that energy will still be there. Your best bet when you move into a new place, even if it is a new built home, you should sage it. Saging will remove all negative energy from the space. You can also call someone to clear and bless the house.

Here is what to do when you live or work with someone who is negative. First stop focusing on the negative. Send baby pink roses and love to this person, affirm that there is peace and harmony between you and that other person. Remember negativity is only a thought and thoughts can be changed. Choose to think positive thoughts only. Protect yourself with the white light or Archangel Michael's light.

We have choices and we can choose negativity or we can choose positivity. Where do you want to be? I choose the positive, better on this side!

Affirmation: I now release all negativity and hold onto to positive.
Negativity bounces off me quickly and easily.
I hold only positive energy within my bubble of light.

0–OILS

Oils are a great tool to use for you, healing work, meditation, massage and many other uses. This is aromatherapy. There are many types of oils and oil blends out there and they all have a purpose.

I always use sage oil to clear the room after a healing session. I need the room clear of any old energy before the next client comes to see me. If the room is not cleared, the next person who comes in can pick up on the old energy and absorb it. Also I need it cleared because after a day of healings and/or readings I don't want the energy either. The sage oil is not used full strength. You mix 10 drops to 8oz. of water in a spray bottle and then just spray the room and area where the healing was done. This is an alternative to burning sage. Some people don't like the small or the smoke so they do the spray instead. The spray has a nice freshening smell, better than store bought and you can clear out your whole house of stagnant old energy.

Lavender is another great oil that I use. Lavender is the best thing for helping you to relax. You can use a drop full strength in your hand and rub your hands together then just breathe in the aroma. Make a spray as well with this one. Add 10 drops to 8oz. of water and spray your bed pillows for a restful sleep. Spray the house for calmness. You can also spray it on dogs (Not near the head) to keep them calm. Another great use is lavender for headaches. Next time you get a headache put one drop at the base of your skull and your headache will disappear.

Lavender oil as well as so many other oils are used in blends. I sell a lot of blends in my gift shop such as angel oil, meditation, spirit guide, goddess oil, protection, chakra oils, crystal oil blends and so many more. Blends can also be made for healing purposes.

Oils can coincide with the chakras, crystals, astrology and feng shui. You can really go all out with oils. I am not an expert with oils but know what I need to know so that I can incorporate it into my healing work. I just wanted to give you a little bit about oils to get you started. Who knows it may be something you would want to take further. Look for aromatherapy classes in your area.

I use a meditation blend that is great for clearing you and helping you to open up. All you have to do is place a drop of meditation blend in your hand, rub hands together then wave your hands over your head from front to back, then wave your hands in a downward motion from the top of your head to your feet clearing away any old energy. Then you can wave your hands around your back as well to clear out behind you. Then just relax and you're ready to meditate.

Here is a small list of different oils and what they are good for.

- **Eucalyptus**—Healing, colds, nasal congestion (do not breathe in directly)
- **Frankincense**—Purification, Luck, Protection, Spirituality
- **Frank & Myrrh**—Protection, Purification, Spirituality
- **Hyssop**—Purification
- **Jasmine**—Spiritual Love
- **Lavender**—Healing, Peace, Love, Relaxation, Headaches
- **Lotus**—Protection, Healing, Spirituality
- **Musk**—Attraction, Lust
- **Myrrh**—Spirituality, Protection
- **Orange**—Love, Beauty, Prosperity
- **Patchouly**—Love, Money, Fertility
- **Patchouly, Dark**—Love, Money, Fertility
- **Pine**—Fertility, Prosperity, Protection
- **Pomegranate**—Divination, Luck, Fertility, Wealth
- **Rose**—Love, Healing, Beauty
- **Rosemary**—Purification, Protection, Healing
- **Sage**—Wisdom, Purification
- **Sandalwood**—Protection, Purification, Spirituality
- **Strawberry**—Love, Good Luck
- **Sweetgrass**—Spiritual Attraction
- **Vanilla**—Love, Lust
- **Violet**—Love, Healing, Peace
- **Wisteria**—Mental Powers
- **Ylang Ylang**—Opportunity, Peace

This list is oils that help with health of skin and hair.

- Basil—To unclog congested sluggish skin, natural insect repellant.
- Cedarwood—Hair care, alopecia, dandruff, skin care.
- Cinnamon—Skin and nail care, tones skin, antiviral in skin and nails.
- Sage—Perk up skin, cell regenerator, stimulates hair growth.
- Eucalyptus—Acne and oily skin, scalp stimulator, antiseptic.
- Frankincense—Calms inflamed skin, good for damaged cuticles.
- Hyssop—Moisturizing skin, treats eczema, weak nails, damaged cuticles
- Jasmine—Reduce oily slick from hair and skin, great for hands and feet.
- Lavender—dry, brittle hair, reduce acne, psoriasis and eczema.
- Oregano—Helps with cellulite, brightens nail beds.
- Sandlewood—Good for nail fungus, dry cracked hands and feet.
- Tea Tree—Dandruff, irritations, acne, nail fungus.

Here are uses for oils that aid in health issues.

- Bergamot—Used especially for mouth, skin, respiratory and urinary tract infections. Bergamot essential oil is useful for anxiety, depression, and stress.
- Cedarwood—Used for nervous tension, anxiety, insomnia, stress, poor circulation, arthritis, rheumatism, respiratory congestion, enhance concentration and zest for life.
- Chamomile—Muscular pain, neuralgia, rheumatism, sprains and burns. Headaches, insomnia, migraine, stress—well known for calming effect on nervous system.
- Cinnamon—Circulation, rheumatism, digestion, spasms, colds, flu. Some use in stress relief. Makes a very warming massage blend—good for rheumatism.
- Clary Sage—Skin care and stress-related conditions including high blood pressure, depression and anxiety. Calms fevers. Good for female system. Good for throat and respiratory infections.

- Clove Bud—Researchers found that sniffing the spicy aroma reduces drowsiness, irritability, and headaches, assists memory recall, and increases circulation. This powerful essential oil also has the ability to abate depression, relieve indigestion, and contribute to sexual stimulations. Skin care and stress-related conditions including high blood pressure, depression and anxiety. Calms fevers. Good for female system. Good for throat and respiratory infections.
- Eucalyptus Lemon—Powerful antiseptic and healing agent. Renowned for treatment of respiratory complaints—often used in inhalants. Can relieve fever and skin irritations. Head-clearing, uplifting, refreshing.
- Geranium, Rose—reducing stress and tension, easing pain, balancing emotions and hormones, PMS, relieve fatigue and nervous exhaustion, to lift melancholy, lessen fluid retention, repel insects. Emotional profile: to aid with acute fear, rigidity, abuse, lack of self-esteem, discontentment, heartache.
- Ginger—muscular problems, arthritis, rheumatism, poor circulation, coughs, sore throat, nausea, travel sickness, colds, flu. Also noted for its decongesting properties.
- Lavender—The most universal of all essential oils. Many uses including skin care, circulation, muscles, joints, digestive, immune system. Sheets washed in lavender are thought to promote sleep.
- Patchouli—Good antiseptic, e.g. minor burns and cracked skin. Calming action. Aphrodisiac.
- Rosemary—Rosemary should be avoided if you are pregnant, if you have epilepsy or high blood pressure. Rosemary is used to energize, for muscle pains, cramps or sprains, brighten mood, for improving mental clarity and memory, easing pain, to relieve headaches, disinfecting.
- Rosewood—Although Rosewood essential oil is not very powerful, it has a place in aromatherapy and could help with the respiratory system, with sexual problems, with stress-related conditions and for skin care.
- Spearmint—Spearmint oil can be effective for the digestive system, for the respiratory tract, for a tired mind and for skin problems. The therapeutic properties of Spearmint oil are: local anesthetic,

antispasmodic, astringent, carminative, decongestant, digestive, diuretic, expectorant, stimulant and restorative.

- Tangerine—calming, cheering, relaxing, soothing, stress, uplifting. Added to Massage Oil, tangerine helps relax cramped muscles. The essential oil is good remedy for premenstrual syndrome, and may be beneficial in treating stomach, liver, and gallbladder problems.
- Tea Tree—Strong antiseptic, anti-inflammatory, anti-bacterial, anti-viral, fungicidal properties. Used for a variety of skin complaints e.g. Athlete's foot, boils, herpes, ulcers, psoriasis, warts.
- Ylang Ylang—Aphrodisiac properties due to intense flowery scent. Anti-depressant. Euphoric qualities. Has a balancing effect on blood pressure and distressed breathing patterns.

As with anything new always do research first. Some oils are not good for pregnant woman. If you are taking any medications always check with your doctor first before using aromatherapy oils. Some oils and medication do not mix.

Aromatherapy can be fun and educational. Find out more by buying a good book on the subject, checking the Internet or find a class in your area.

P—PAST LIFE

A Past Life is a life that you lived before this life now here on earth. We have all lived many many lives. Some more than others. That is what we call an old soul.

We live our life to learn certain lessons that we have implemented into the contract we made before we came to live on the earthly plane. We live our lives, learning as we go along and if we do not complete all the lessons we set out to accomplish and learn from them, them we come back to live another life. It is like school. If you don't pass agreed you have to repeat it until you do pass. We choose to come back over and over again to learn for our soul. I just pray I got it right this time. I have spent enough time here. I'm ready to be a guide for someone else.

Once we are born into a new life, we have no recollection of our past life. Although there are times when we have those déjà vu moments. This is that feeling you get when you feel like "I have been here before". When in fact you haven't in this life. More than likely you are experiencing a moment of time from a past life. There a some cell memories that get stuck in our subconscious and when we step into a scenery or meet someone new we feel like we have done this already.

Past life can also wreak havoc on our physical and mental bodies as well. Cell memory can also be pain, sickness, fears, phobias and other issues that turn up out of nowhere. Here is an example: I had worked with a client that had this strange issue. Every time she would put her face down in a pillow, in a massage cradle or had a cold with a stuffy nose, she thought she was suffocating. So when she brought this to my attention, right away I heard past life issue. You see she never had this problem until she turned 42 years old. So I talked with her about doing past life regression and she agreed. During the session I brought her back to her previous life. Once there I brought her back to the age of 42. Then she suddenly started getting anxious. When I asked her what was going on, she told me there was a man present and that he snuck up behind her and with a cloth, placed it over her mouth and nose and smothered her until she died. I reassured her that what happened was in a past life and she can let it go and that in her current life now she is perfectly safe and she can breathe easy. She was so much better after that and didn't feel that smothering feeling any more.

Other things that can come through into a new life are birthmarks, skin discolorations, phantom pain and other markings on the body. In a book that I read about past life one man was put under and brought into his passed life. Turned out he was living in the jungle with his tribe. Then one day another tribe waged war with his. During the fight he was hit with a spear in his thigh. When he was brought out of hypnosis he showed the person that was working with him the skin discoloration on his thigh, right in the place he described during his past life regression. So your birthmarks and skin discolorations mean more than you think.

Phantom pain can be from a past life. Have you ever had a pain that just happened out of nowhere and you go to the doctors only for him/her to tell you that they didn't find anything? Same as the example above. You may have endured something painful in your past life and your cell memory is now bringing it up to you. Using past life regression can help with this or call upon Archangel Michael to help you let go of past life cell memory so you can live a healthy pain free life.

People can share past lives too. Have you ever had such a connection with someone here in this life? You feel more like sisters than friends, you feel like you have known them forever and have so much in common. It can be true for couples as well. Some couples are just so meant to be together. You look at these two people and you wish you could have the connection that they have. Here is example: my daughter told me when she was very small that she was my mother in a past life. Well that has to be true because for a 10 year old, she is very domesticated and tells everyone what to do. I mean really, what 10 year old do you know, calls you at work and asks how to run the washing machine? I was laughing.

A reader told me that my three children all shared a passed life together and promised that they would share the next one too. I have a picture that was given to me by this person that shows the three of them. In this picture there is one boy, two girls but not twins. One was much smaller than the other. Today I have three children. A son, a set of twin girls and one is much smaller than the other. They look like sisters, but not twins. Pretty good match to the picture.

Regressing someone can also be to bring them back into their past of this life now. There are times when something tragic happened when they were younger and it is now having an impact on them now as an adult.

What happens is when a person goes through a tragic event they tend to bury it in their subconscious instead of expressing it and letting it go. As the years go by the issue is still there butt is now eating away at them, and as I said earlier emotions can and will become physical issues. So through regression I can bring someone back to that tragic time. Help them to see it, acknowledge it and then finally release it and let it go.

How do you know if this is something you need? Well once someone comes to see me for whatever issue they are trying to heal my intuition kicks in and I am guided to whether they need hypnosis or regression. Also many people know they experienced something when they were younger but can't recall it completely, so they may specifically ask for regression to see what is in their subconscious.

Letting go of the past is very important. When you do let go you clear out your body, mind and soul and are balanced. When you hold onto the past everything just gets backed up. You get worse emotionally, mentally, physically and spiritually. Your soul cannot progress. Think of it like this: you don't clean your house; you let the garbage pile up. You know it needs cleaning but you don't acknowledge it. Your hoping it will just go away. The longer you keep this up, the worse it gets. More trash, more dirt, more work to get it done. Now it is to the point that you can't live there any longer it is so filthy. Now the only way you could stay is if you clean it, but now it is so bad that you feel helpless and don't know what to do. You can't do it alone and you now need help. The past is the same; you hold onto it, don't acknowledge it and now you're a emotional mess. You need help to let go or you may never recover.

Now I'm sure no of you live like this but why is it we can keep our things in order but not ourselves. Take care of yourself and keep a balance in your body, mind and soul. Think about it if your child was ill you would be doing everything possible to make sure they received the care they needed no matter the time or money. So why is it when we need care, we ignore it. We always seem to put our stuff on the back burner, like we don't matter. You do matter so keep your "House" clean, let go of the old stuff and fill yourself with light and love. If you feel you need help to clear things out then get it. Let go and let God!

Affirmations: I now release _____ from my past and live in the present and move forward.
I now take care of myself, so that I am balanced in my mind, body and soul. I live a healthy life.

P—PRIORITIES

Priorities are people and things in our lives that we put in order of importance. I find that with many people I work with they have everyone and everything on their list except themselves or they always seem to put themselves at the very bottom of the list. I will always ask my clients where they are on their priority list and they usually tell me somewhere at the bottom or not even on the list. I tell them and I'm telling you, you need to be at the top of your list. You need to take care of yourself. Some think it is selfish, but it isn't. Putting yourself first just to snub others and think they are less important than you is selfish.

We need to take care of ourselves. We need to do things that we enjoy. Now I don't mean do everything you enjoy and totally neglect other important things but do take the time to do for you. A lot of people don't do this especially women. We tend to feel we need to take of everything and everybody. I think it is part of our genetics. I know I used to feel like I needed to take care of my husband, children, the house, the chores, errands, bills, pets, friends, job, and then maybe me. By the time I did all this there was no time for me or I was way too tired to do anything except sleep. When we do this we get run down and eventually get sick. It is our body's way of slowing us down.

All these demands on out time take a toll on our emotional, mental, physical and spiritual bodies. Are you one of those people who have your head spinning constantly? Do you have trouble sleeping because your brain never shuts down? You are allowing these demands on your time to take over. You need to stop this vicious cycle. Sit down and write what your priorities are, starting with you. Be sure to add your faith first . . . God is very important and with out him/her we wouldn't be here. Then continue with what is important in your life that you need to take care of. Here is my priority list:

1.God
2.Me
3.Family (spouse, children, extended family)
4.Work
5.Friends
6.and so on.

I now make sure that I take care of me. I let go of the guilt that I used to have when I did things for me. I know that I need that time for me. I now enjoy meditating, get out alone, go out with the girls, take a class or do whatever else I feel is good for me. Before all this when I felt guilty, I would stay home and miss out on a lot and everyone at home was happy that mom stayed home, except me. I had to change this and get everyone to understand that I needed to have "ME" time. Everyone needs "Me" time. We all need that time of peace and quiet now and then.

Find time everyday to do something for yourself, whether it is to meditate, read a book, go for a walk, have a hobby or whatever else makes you happy. You will see once you start doing for you everything seems to be better. Your energy rises up. Those around you will understand even if it takes them a little while.

Affirmation: I now take time for me everyday to do ＿＿＿＿＿＿.
          My loved ones understand and are supportive of my me time.

Q—QUIET TIME

Quiet time is something we all need to allow our minds to let go of the daily grind and have some peace and quiet. Getting some quiet time is not only a priority, like I just discussed but also a healthy way of letting go. Many people have so much going on in their lives and they keep it all on their minds or they fill their minds with the daily chores for the next day.

You have to take some time to clear your mind daily in order to let go of what went on that day, even if you only have a few minutes to do it. Holding onto all this is not healthy for your body or mind. For your mind, there is no rest and the body gets no rest either because the mind is still going so much that more than likely you are not sleeping well. This is holding onto the past, even if it was only a hour ago, it is the past. You have to let it go, don't absorb it and let it take your mind over.

Worrying about what needs to be done tomorrow is wasting energy on the future. I ask people all the time, "If you worry about it does it change it"? The answer is no. It is a natural thing to have some worry we are all human. Dwelling in it is wasted energy. Use that energy to be positive and create a better outcome. Don't worry about things that are not even here yet.

Taking quiet time for yourself may not be easy at first but you need to work at it just like everything else. They say it takes 21 days to create a new habit, so keep up the practice. You will then get to a point where you wonder how you ever managed without your quiet time. First you need to find a quiet place even if you have to lock yourself in the bathroom for ten minutes. Now like meditation, close your eyes and take three deep breaths and just be. Relax and let things go. You probably will have thoughts come to your mind, just acknowledge them then let them go. You can also call in Archangel Michael to help you to let go of what you no longer need.

Just like an engine that has been running all day, you have to shut it down and let it cool down. Otherwise it will over heat and break down. You are the same way. Overwork yourself emotionally, physically and mentally and you too will break down, so to say. When you don't take care of yourself by getting some quiet time, your body will react. Those who are always on the go, let everything bother them, hold onto the past, and never take time to cool down, will eventually get sick either by getting a cold, the flu or some other ailment. Pay attention to what your body is telling you. Our bodies warn us when we need to slow down and take some quiet time. If you ignore this, the universe will step in and make something happen to make you slow down. So please take those few minutes everyday to let go, clear your mind, let go of worry about tomorrow, live in the present and just be . . . quiet.

Affirmations: I take time daily to be quiet and clear my mind.
I always take time to clear my mind for my health.
I live in the present moment now and always.

R—REIKI

Reiki is a hands on healing art that has been around for centuries. Dr. Mikao Usui rediscovered it in the early 1900's in Japan. Dr. Usui was a teacher in a Christian school. His students asked him one day about how Jesus did laying of hands and how they could do it. He could not answer them, so this is when he decided to go on his quest to find the answers. Dr. Usui traveled all over to search for the answers, reading all religious text that he could find, still with no answers. Then during the early 1920s, Usui did a 21-day practice on Mount Kurama. This is where he had been given the inspiration for his system of healing—Reiki. This was just the beginning to Usui's Reiki healing that quickly became world known. It is practiced everywhere in the world. Here in the USA it is becoming more and more popular. Many use it as a compliment to traditional medicine.

There are many different forms of Reiki practiced and taught and I am only going to write about the traditional Usui system that I learned and now teach. I am a Reiki Master/Teacher and as of now I have been practicing Reiki for almost 7 years. I love doing Reiki and the results I have seen from it truly are amazing. I have worked with many clients throughout these past few years and some of the ailments that have improved with Reiki are cancer, arthritis, anxiety, bi-polar, emotional issues, pain, discomfort, post traumatic stress disorder (PTSD), insomnia, balance of the chakra system and so much more. I do have those who come in just for the pure relaxation that Reiki can bring someone.

There is so much healing that can take place during a session. My clients have experienced emotional release, pain healed and clarity to their mind. Depending on a persons ailments or issues depends on how much Reiki they will need. Someone who has pain may only need one session. Those who are dealing with deeper issues or illness will need more than one session. Usually I will have them come back weekly or bi-weekly until things have cleared. Now I never promise any miraculous healings with

Reiki. I never know what will happen. You may have some healing but not full healing. I know first hand that Reiki can do so much for people and I wish it would always heal everyone completely, but I truly believe that it up to you and what you contracted for yourself before you came to this earth plain.

The great thing about Reiki is that it can heal something as simple as a headache all the way to a major disease. I remember one day while volunteering at the hospital, one of the workers was complaining of a headache. So I asked if I could do Reiki for her and she said yes. Five minutes of Reiki and her headache was gone. Another worker was really stressed out. I told her to sit for five minutes. I did the Reiki and then had her take a deep breath and when I moved my hands, she said it felt like all the stress was pulled right off of her. Needless to say she felt so much better.

Here is another example of healing through Reiki. I had a client who wanted Reiki for anxiety. She explained that she has not slept a full night in 15 years, she has been to the doctors, test were run and nothing came out of the results. All he did was give her medication to sleep. So I explained the Reiki to her and proceeded to do the session with her. After I was done, she asked what I did because she felt so much better, like things were let go. I had also seen a man in spirit who she recognized when I told her. It was someone who she still had emotional distress with. I gave her the message he told me. She was in shock, because she thought that since he was no longer with us, she was over the issues with him. She then booked another appointment with me for the following week. The next day my phone rang and it was she. She then asked me what I did to her. I was confused and asked her why. She told me that I did for her what no doctor could. The doctor never found anything wrong. Of course an x-ray or MRI cannot see emotional distress. She had slept all night long and felt better than ever. She was very thankful and continued to see me until she felt herself again.

People ask me if I get tired after doing Reiki because I am using my energy to help others. Well the truth is, it is not my energy. The energy I pass to others is God's energy (or what ever source you work with). When I am going to practice Reiki, the first thing I do is call on God to send his/her loving, healing, positive energy through me to the person I am working on. I then place my hands on the person in different areas from head to feet. This allows the energy to flow through them and bring healing to any areas of emotional or physical pain and discomfort. The Reiki energy will also align and balance the persons chakra system.

What a client feels during a Reiki session is always relaxation, but can also feel emotions come to the surface. They may start crying and not know why but this is a release. They may feel the energy moving through them. They will feel my hands get warm to hot in certain areas of the body. They can feel tingling, vibration and even see flashing lights or colors while their eyes are closed. Some don't see anything and that is Ok. It doesn't mean it is not working. Everyone experiences Reiki differently.

What I feel during a Reiki session is similar. My hands will be warm to very hot. I feel vibration and tingling in different areas. I have also had my hands go ice cold, which I learned is a way I pick up on old injuries. One young lady I worked with, my hand s went cold over her right shoulder. When I asked her about it, she told me that she had broken the color bone on that side when she was a kid. Intuition is my other tool aside from my hands. I follow the guidance I am given during the session. For example when my hands are on someone's heart and there is indication of something wrong, right away I will know if it a physical issue or emotional through my intuition. I also listen for messages from loved one's in spirit, guides, angels or anyone else from the higher vibrations of light. I at times will feel the pain the person I am working on feels. It is only long enough for me to know what is wrong.

I don't work alone during my sessions. I love my Angels and always call on them for help with my sessions. I call on anyone and everyone from the higher vibrations to help. It is funny at times when I am working with a client and they tell me after the session that they could feel someone else touching them while I was in a different area of their body. The room usually gets very warm with all the energy in there and the angels.

Reiki can last for a while with someone after they leave my office depending on how severe the issues or pain. Some have noticed that the Reiki really kicked in later on after they left my office. I had one client that had a hip issue and after the session, the hip still hurt. I told her to wait and that the Reiki will push it's way through and help her. Well about two hours later she said her hip popped and the pain was gone. Sometimes people's energy can get stuck and it takes some time for the Reiki to work through it.

Reiki can also be done through distance healing. When I hear of someone who is ill or going through a tough time I will ask him or her if I can send healing and then I do so through distance Reiki. This is done by using Reiki, the Reiki symbols and intention. This works well with those who cannot come into the office, those who live far away, someone going in for surgery and so on.

Reiki can speed up the healing process too. When someone is going in for surgery, I will send Reiki once it is over. The Reiki makes healing happen faster. When my son was 6 years old, he had his tonsils out. When the nurse let me into recovery I started doing Reiki right away. I could see the energy moving all around his neck and into his nose because he had his adenoids taken out too. I saw the color green all over these areas (green is the color of healing). Normally after tonsil surgery you cannot eat. You have to have things that are cold and soft. Usually liquids the first day then onto soft foods there after until healed. Well my son ate a ham sandwich the very next day. It was small pieces and he ate slowly, but he was able to eat. He also had no pain. He started school just four days later. It was great!

I love doing Reiki for people. I love to see people heal from their issues or ailments. I also teach Reiki. There are three levels to learn, but you don't have to do all three. You can learn just the first level and do healings. Reiki I is learning the history of Reiki, what it is, how it works, how to do it for yourself and others, grounding, protection and you receive an attunement so that you can pass the energy. Reiki II is learning the Reiki symbols and how to do distance healings. You receive another attunement as well. Reiki III Master/Teacher is learning the master symbol, learning how to teach Reiki and how to do attunements. You receive you final attunement. All three levels a student will receive a certificate of completion.

People tell me that I must have a special gift to be able to do what I do. You don't need or have to have a special gift; we can all do this work. All you need is the will to learn and the compassion to heal those in need. If you have never had Reiki before, I suggest you try at least once, so you can see the benefits. You will be surprised at how you feel afterwards.

Reiki and religion must be written in here. Reiki IS NOT part of any religion what so ever. People assume that it is because I say I channel the energy from God. God is part of many religions but this is not religious at all. Some think Reiki is Buddhist but is not. Just because Usui was a

Buddhist it doesn't mean Reiki is. Believe me many people practice Reiki and they all come from different backgrounds and beliefs.

At this time the only religion that has an issue with Reiki is the Catholic Church. They tell their people that we spread evil energy and work with the devil. In 2009 The Arch diocese of Conn. And Mass denounced Reiki and said there will be no practice of it in any of their churches, health care facilities, schools and so on. Well I have done Reiki on many Catholics and other faiths and I haven't killed anyone yet. I just think that they are being ignorant. They say you can't prove Reiki (sorry, wrong. It has been tested) the only real healings are divine healings through the church. Well I would like to know how they prove that. Any way, take what you want from what I have written and whatever you don't agree with, toss it aside. Always go with what feels right in your heart, not anyone else's.

R—REFLEXOLOGY

Reflexology is a practice of using the pressure points in the hands and feet to promote healing within the body giving a calm and intentional message to the nervous system to improve or correct physical and emotional stresses.

Reflexology is an ancient technique of applying pressure to reflex points of the feet and hands. This ancient healing art has been traced back to ancient China. Archeologists have found stone-carved stone reflexology charts of Buddha's feet dating to around 40 B.C. For more background on the history of reflexology see Sokushin Do History.

Foot reflexology later traveled to Japan during the Tang dynasty and spread in other parts of Asia such as present day Korea and Thailand. Egyptian hieroglyphics discovered in the tomb of Ankhmahor, a ka-priest from 2400 BC, depict a foot and hand reflexology treatment in progress.

Foot Reflexology became part of mainstream medical therapy in India, and flourished in European countries such as Germany where the course of study is comparable to that of a medical physician. Reflexology eventually found its way to America and was popularized when Eunice Ingham published her best-selling book, "Stories The Feet Can Tell".

The reflexology pressure points found on the hands and feet act as a map for healing the anatomy. Knowledge of these maps has been preserved by many cultures throughout history.

Reflexology is a complimentary therapy, which works on the whole person not just the prevailing symptoms. It can be used to help restore and maintain the body's natural equilibrium. This gentle therapy encourages the body to work naturally to restore its own healthy balance. Has been shown to be effective for: Back pain, migraines, infertility, arthritis, sleep disorders, sports injury, and more. While many people use Reflexology as a way of relaxing the mind and body and counteracting stress, at the same time many doctors, consultants and other health care professionals recognize Reflexology as a well established, respected and effective therapy.

The systematic application of pressure to the reflexology points stimulates the body's ability to rejuvenate and heal itself. Hand and Foot Reflexology treatments open the subtle electrical channels that become blocked due to emotional and physical imbalances.

Creating a physiological change in the body improving circulation and thereby reducing stress, reflexology aids in the elimination of body waste and restores body function to improve health.

Working on a cellular level to rebalance the body, nourish the cells with nutrients, alter the cellular memory of emotions, and change the electrical vibration in a way that allows the body to process food efficiently and detoxify naturally.

What are the benefits of reflexology?

- Creates relaxation: From the moment the reflexologist's hands start their work, the relaxation begins.
- Reduces pain: Pain reduction following reflexology work
- Ameliorates health concerns: Research shows that reflexology work helps individuals of all ages with some 78 health concerns ranging from aggressive behavior in children to urinary concerns of the elderly.
- Improves blood flow: studies show that reflexology work increases blood flow to the feet, brain, kidneys and intestines.
- Aids post-operative recovery: Reflexology work aids recovery after surgery as shown by several studies, reducing pain and lessening the use of post operative analgesics.
- Impact on physiological measures (e. g. blood pressure and cholesterol; measurements by ECG, EEG, and MRI)
- Enhances medical care: Reflexology helps where nothing else can for many: phantom limb pain sufferers, neuropathy patients, and hemodialysis patients to name a few.
- Benefits mental health: Research demonstrates that reflexology can reduce depression and anxiety.
- Complements cancer care: Pain, nausea, vomiting, and/or anxiety eased for chemotherapy patients following reflexology work as shown by16 studies from 7 countries.
- Eases pregnancy, delivery and post-partum effects: Women who received reflexology experienced shorter labor times and used less

analgesia. In addition, reflexology showed a positive impact on postpartum depression, anxiety, urination and bowel movements.

In general terms, the benefits of reflexology have to do with the reduction of stress. Because the feet and hands help set the tension level for the rest of the body, they are an easy way to interrupt the stress signal and reset homeostasis, the body's equilibrium.

Reflexology is a complement to standard medical care. It should not be construed as medical advice. It should not be a replacement to medical help.

S—SACRED SPACE

Sacred Space is a place that you create. It is a place meant for you to sit quietly, meditate, journal or do healing work. A sacred space can be a room in your house, a corner in a room, even a large walk in closet or a professional office space that you rent for your healing work.

When people come to our healing center, they immediately feel peace. My sister and I have created a place of positive serenity, where they can come to relax, heal and get inspired. We have clients that stop in just to have a cup of tea or coffee and just talk with us. By the time they are ready to leave they feel so much better. It makes my heart smile when people walk in and the first thing out of their mouth is "I love this place it is so peaceful". We have created a beautiful sacred space for us and our clients.

At my home I have a three season room that I have set up just for me to sit quiet. My sacred space is filled with many different items that I enjoy and bring me peace. I have sage, crystals, sea salt, angels, candles, oils and my meditation music. This is where I go when I need to recharge. I use this room because in my home it is a little busy with my husband and three children, a little hard to be alone.

How do you create your own sacred space? First you need to find a space in your home. It could be a separate room in your home, a corner of a room, A large closet (Like a walk in closet), in your basement, an outside room (like a sun porch) or any other available space you have.

Next you need to set it up according to what feels good to you. Have a comfortable chair or pillow to sit on the floor, a small table if you have one and then start putting decorations that help you get into your peaceful place. You could use crystals, candles, sage, incense, statues (angels, Jesus, Mother Mary, Buddha, Kwan Yin, etc.) salt lamps or selenite lamps, aromatherapy oils, meditation music and a journal to write down your experiences, your thoughts, dreams, goals and anything else you want to add.

After you get everything set up you will need to place your intentions and energy into your space. Start by saging the area. Use either the burning type sage or the sage spray. As you sage, ask God that all lower energies or entities be taken up into the light and that your area be filled with positive love, light and energy. Be sure to sage the whole outer edge of your space and everything in between.

How to sage: whenever you feel the need to cleanse or purify yourself, a room, an object or another person, you can perform a smudging ritual. Smudging is a Native American ritual used in purification ceremonies to cleanse and balance the aura or energies of people, places and objects. To smudge, light a smudge stick, or a densely packed bundle of dried sage herbs. The lit sage bundle produces a cloud of fragrant smoke that you can waft around a person or place that needs spiritual cleansing.

Open a window or a door so that any negative energy can find a way out of the room. Focus your intention on cleansing the energy in the room. Light one end of your sage smudge stick with a match and place the smudge stick on a heat-resistant plate. The embers of the sage will produce smoke. If your sage is burning with an open flame, blow out the flame so that the embers remain. Walk slowly around the room with the plate, using your hands to wave the smoke from the sage throughout the room. Walk around the room a final time with your smudge stick. Attract positive energies into the room by focusing your intention on creating a purified and spiritual place.

Now you need to place your intensions. Call in Archangel Michael and ask him to surround your space in his light and protect it and you from outside energies. Then sit quiet for a moment and take a couple of deep breaths. Call on God, your guides and Angels into your space and say: This is my own space where only good intentions, love light, peace and serenity are allowed and may this space be filled with God's light. Now visualize your space filled with pure white light.

You now have a sacred space all your own. The more you use it the more your energy will fill the space. So much so that when you are in different rooms of you house, you will be able to feel the difference in energy. Be sure to explain to others in your home that this is your space for mediation and they should respect that by staying out. I call it my time out room. If you live with someone who is on the spiritual level as you, then by all means make the space for both of you where you can meditate and connect together. It is all up to you.

Most important! Have fun making and creating your space. Make it all your own!

Affirmation: I now have a sacred space all my own where I can meditate and take time for myself.
I now sit in my sacred space daily where I can recharge my energy.

S—SPIRITUAL COUNSELING

Spiritual Counseling is a group session that I hold at my center with my Spiritual friend Lorianne. We hold it every other week and it is open to everyone. We do not charge for this group, we feel that this group is meant to help those who seek it and many can't afford to continuously pay for help. We do accept donations, some feel that they would like to give back.

During this group we help others to learn how to be more positive, get through tough times, learn how to let go, forgiveness or how to work on building their own spirituality. People ask me all the time "what is spiritual counseling"? I tell them it is a place where you can come and talk about the good, the bad and the ugly or you can just sit and listen till you're ready to open up. Whatever is comfortable for that person. Many of my people come because they enjoy being with likeminded people. We also talk about guides, angels, ascended master and loved ones on the other side on how they help us. Lorianne and I are intuitive so if we receive messages from the other side we pass it along to whomever it is for.

There has and continues to be a great assortment of people who come to the group. We have mostly women, but there are few men that have and continue to come. Everyone comes from different backgrounds but they all have the same intention, to see things in a better light.

Other discussions we have can include alternative therapies like massage, Reiki, Theta or Divine energy healings for those to receive, if it seems like they need more than just talking in a group.

We always start the group with everyone picking an Angel card for a message. Most of the time as soon as they look at the card they know exactly what it means. The cards usually coincide with what is going on with them at the time. Sometimes a person doesn't understand their card so we tell them to wait and by the time the group session is over they will understand what the card means. I will also help them to understand what the Angels are trying to tell them. Angel cards are a great way to stay on track. You don't have to know how to read cards to do it. Get yourself a deck and everyday just pick one as a message for the day. The cards are amazing and the messages are so helpful.

Some of the discussed issues that we have helped people with are:

- How to let go
- How to manifest
- How to be more positive
- How to forgive
- Looking at everything with love
- People going through a divorce
- Keeping people positive during illness and disease
- People going through grief
- Breaking free from negativity
- Saying goodbye to those who have passed
- Family issues
- Marriage issues
- And so much more . . .

The great thing about the group is not only do Lorianne and I help he group, but the group helps each other. Many times there will be someone in the group that has gone through the same issue someone is speaking of and they help each other. One may tell the other how they got through their rough time. So we all help each other out. It is a great thing.

The most important thing in our group is that it is completely confidential. Everyone signs a confidentiality paper when they first come and it is understood that we do not tolerate gossip outside the group at all! What is said during the group stays in the group. I want people to trust me and know that they are safe when they come for group. Sisters of Solace is not a place of negativity. We are there to help all who seek it.

This is also a fun group, we laugh, we cry and we learn to let go of what no longer serves us. For me it makes my heart sing o know that people are receiving the help they need. I know this is my purpose in life and it feels good!

So if you live in my area, stop in and see us. If not, find a center in your area that offers Spiritual Counseling. It is a great way to clear your mind, body and soul.

T—TRUST

Trust is having the faith that whatever you are seeking will happen. Trust is also having the faith that those in your life are true to what they say and do. So many have issues with trust. They don't listen to their own intuition, they have issues with love because they have been hurt before, there are past life issues if trust that follow people into this life or for whatever other reason just don't trust anyone.

Trust is a tough one for people who don't listen to their own intuition. They feel that since they are not a professional reader or psychic, their intuition can't be right. How many times have you had a gut feeling and went against it because you didn't trust yourself or your feelings? People tell me all the time that they knew something was wrong, felt that something was wrong or the most popular, my gut told me something was wrong and they didn't follow through. You have to learn to trust. Even for myself, it took a while for me to completely trust my own intuition. Especially when the information you are getting doesn't make sense right away.

During my healing work I had to learn to trust the information as well. My guides were giving me messages and I would think that I was just thinking it in my head. I had to learn that the messages were real and I had to pass them on no matter what. If they didn't make sense that was all right because the message was for the person I was working on, not me. I finally came to realize that if God put me in this position to do his work, then I could trust the information that came with it. If I was wrong in giving a message, it was ok, not everyone was right 100% of the time. Even the most famous of psychics are not right 100% of the time.

So how do you learn to trust? Just do it. Write down everything you get that you think is a message or a feeling about someone or something. You decide to go with it or not and then go back and check what you wrote and see if you were right or not. The more you see how much you are right the more you will trust.

When you don't trust, you are letting your ego get in the way. That little voice in your head that is negative and tells you:

- Your just making it up
- You can't
- That's not right
- Your hearing things
- And so on

That is when you have to tell your ego to be quiet and go with your thoughts, feelings, visions or hearing. This is called trusting through your heart not your head.

Another trust issue people have is not trusting others. This may be due to the fact that someone has given them a reason not to trust. Such as:

- Crossed you some way
- Cheated you financially
- Cheated romantically
- Lied to you
- Stole from you
- And so on

This is a tough thing to go through, but this is also a lesson. This is where you have to learn to let go and trust that everything will turn out fine and the person who did this to you will have to deal with their karma. I know this is easier said than done. Many immediately put a wall as soon as they are hurt in some way. This is not a good thing to do. What happens is the next person who comes into your life is going to have to fight with that wall you put up. You can't assume that every person you meet is going to give you a reason to not trust them. If you keep that wall up, you will not be able to attract more people into your life. Use your intuition, trust what it is telling you and you will be fine. Let that wall down a little at a time and you will learn to trust.

Now you might be saying that you have been hurt over and over and that everyone you meet gives you a reason not to trust. I want you to look at the people you are choosing to let into your life. Do they all have the same qualities? Do you see a pattern here? People will tell me "I seem to attract these kind of people". Well then it is time to change the way you attract people. Remember what you put out there is exactly what you are going to get back. So change what it is your looking for. Instead of thinking that "I always attract these kind of people", try saying I AM attracting people who are loving, trustworthy and perfect for me. This will help you to get what you want and now you just have to trust that these people will come your way.

God is another one to blame to when things go wrong. Right away people lose their trust in God during bad times. People say that they have prayed and God didn't answer. Not so, he answers everyone's prayers. The problem is we don't hear the answers or we are so tied up in the drama in the situation that there is no way guidance will get through. There are times when we have to go through tough times in life because it is a life's lesson and we have to figure things out on our own. Then things can change for the better. You have to learn to trust that everything happens for a reason and you have the choice of letting the drama get the best of you or taking control of your life and fixing things. When God gives you thoughts or messages, trust it and go with it. Many times people get the guidance but don't trust it and things just don't get better. Trust, Trust, Trust. God, Angels, Guides and all those from the higher vibrations would never steer you in the wrong direction.

I remember when I was married to my first Husband we ran into financial hardship and I remember asking God to please help us. I prayed that we would have extra money so we could pay the rent and other bills. Well to my amazement two days later the landlord called and offered my ex husband a job doing maintenance for all the apartments and if he accepted he would take $150.00 off the rent. I was so happy. My ex said yes and what a big help that was. You see I asked and trusted that God would come through and he did. This all happened way before I got into my spiritual work, but even then I trusted that if it was meant to be it would be fine and it was.

Affirmations: I now trust my intuition.
I have faith and trust that I will be cared for.
I now let go of fear and fully trust.

T–THETA HEALING

Theta Healing is a healing modality developed by Vianna Stibal that allows the practitioner to facilitate instant changes in a client's physical body and belief systems.Theta Healing is essentially applied quantum physics. Using a theta brain wave, which until now was believed to be accessible only in deep sleep or yogi-level meditation, the practitioner is able to connect with the energy of All That Is to identify issues with and witness healings on the physical body, and to identify and change limiting beliefs.

Theta is the brain wave frequency we are in while we are asleep dreaming, or in a state of deep hypnosis. The Orion Technique utilizes the theta brain state to pull and correct negative core beliefs. In other words, conscious or unconscious beliefs that have blocked your ability to succeed in areas which are important to you—love, career, health—and replaces them with a belief system that supports your goals and needs. It can be useful for anything from the removal of a disease to improved mental health and well-being.

In Theta Healing (as taught by Vianna Stibal) the practitioner through prayer and accessing a 'theta state' works with the co-creative force of God by asking God to find the dysfunction or 'dis-ease' in the body, show us the cause and ask God to correct the problem. The practitioner is there to be a witness to the changes made in the body. Recurring 'dis-ease' can be due to several reasons, among them being core belief issues that manifest the 'dis-ease' originally or constant exposure to Toxins.

Core Beliefs:

Core beliefs are programs that run the body. Our brain is like a super computer that maintains our body, shapes our perceptions and reacts to the outside world based upon the core belief programs. We react to life based upon our core belief programs. For example: The program "I'm stupid"—this could come from a simple offhand remark from parents to a child who spilt their milk and a parent or authority figure out of frustration says . . . "why are you so stupid, watch what your doing". The child under the age of six has very little or no discernment about the "TRUTH" of what is being said around them, their mind assumes that the parent knows everything and they must be stupid. So now the child has in their subconscious mind the program "I'm stupid". As the child grows up they may accept the program of "I'm stupid" and act accordingly to perpetuate this program of not doing well in school for example, or they may want to disprove this by working harder to not be seen as 'stupid' but it will be harder for them. They may do well in school and be told how smart they are, which now creates conflicting programs in the brain of "I'm smart" and "I'm stupid".

These conflicting or dual belief programs may stop a person from taking action in their life, or they may do things to facilitate both programs. In this case, they do well in school but they unconsciously do other things which result in them saying to themselves "I'm so stupid why did I do that". How many of us hear ourselves saying that?

Listening to our Self-Talk shows us what kinds of programs are running in our brain and how the negative ones stop us from getting where we want to be in life. This is called self-sabotage, purposefully doing things subconsciously to block getting what we want.

Theta Healing can be a great way to open doors by removing negative programs, which allow us to move forward and achieve what we want in life.

These programs come from 4 sources—1) subconscious programs, 2) genetic programs, 3) deep genetic programs, 4) soul level.

1. Subconscious Programs: The example just given above is an example of how programs can get in our subconscious as a child, they also can come from repetition or poor discernment later in life—i.e. believing everything about your self that other people say about you.

    Another example of this is: Two brothers are told by their father "your stupid and will never amount to anything", the one brother works hard against this program, using his free will, he becomes wealthy and successful. The other brother resigns himself into believing in that program and never tries to succeed at anything. As adults both of them still have the program running. The successful brother can never relax and enjoy his life, because he is always fighting against the program since he is afraid of being a failure. Using the theta technique to cancel the negative program and replace it with "I'm successful, I deserve to be successful", allows the successful brother to relax and enjoy the fruits of his labor. The other brother now has to take action to be successful, but is obviously harder for him because he has not had the practice of doing things to become successful. This brother would need coaching of some sort to get his mind to shift around a new paradigm.

2. Genetic programs: These are programs for everything from eye color, to the way talk, these are intuitions and there are programs similar to subconscious programs above. How these come from your parents DNA and their parents DNA and so on. So many of these programs can be very out dated. They may have been necessary 300 years ago—like the program "I need to hide" so that a person during that day and age wasn't killed, but would be stopping you from enjoying life now. There are also a lot of religious based programs from other time periods which are not very loving—e.g. "God's a punish God", "I'm a sinner, I need to be punished", "I don't deserve to live". Such programs could be a reason a person's body has accepted a disease like cancer. These programs as well as deep genetic programs tend to be the causative effect of predisposing our body to an illness or a disease. These programs may need to be cancelled in order for the body to rid itself of the disease.

3. Deep Genetic Programs: Are similar to genetic programs but go much further back in the DNA and may be what is termed a 'past life'. A person who remembers a past life—may be picking up on their own genetic line, which they lived then or it may be a past life, which is not related genetically.

4. Soul Level Programs: These are deep programs which are carried with the soul. Most of the programs that influence our lives are not on the soul level, but if they are they can have profound effects on our lives and health.

U–UNDOING OLD BELIEF SYSTEMS

Undoing Old Belief Systems can be difficult for some people. We are brought and taught to believe what we are told by our parents, schools and religions. Then for what ever reason, as we get older we start to question what we have been told. We feel that there is more out there or our hearts begin to tell us otherwise. I believe we have to go with what feels right in our hearts. That is truth.

When I was a child all the way up to teenager I had to go to church and catechism and I never felt right about it. I didn't like what I was hearing but I did my part and went up to confirmation. After that I never went back and my parents understood. My grandparents on the other hand were not very happy. They were devout Catholics and truly believed that if you didn't go to church, you would end up in hell. I just couldn't do it.

Now I call myself Spiritual and do not belong to any organized religion. Church is where ever I am and talk with God. If you love to go to church that is fine. Some feel better being in church. They may feel like they connect better. We are entitled to what ever we feel right for us. I am open to all beliefs.

For those who feel like there is more out there, you have to go with your heart, what makes you happy and feels right to you. This is part of letting go and undoing an old belief system.

Now I have talked to many people over that past few years who tell me that if they change their ways and follow what they believe, their parents or someone else would be mad. So out of fear they stay with what they were told and are not happy or filled spiritually. I know this can be hard, but you have to do what is right for you and as far as the other person who may get mad, they need to learn to respect your wishes. It doesn't change you as a person, you're just a person with a different point of view.

This is where you need to take what you have read in this book and apply it. First: Put yourself first, Second: Do what makes you happy,

Third: Let go of the fear and the ego and just trust! Those around you will eventually get over it and if not, it is their issue not yours. It really is OK to have your own beliefs and be happy. Do Not stay in a space that makes you unhappy just so others will be happy.

So how do you change your old belief systems? There are different ways to do this.

- One is to affirm everyday what it is you do believe until it becomes completely comfortable and true without guilt.
- Reiki is also a way to change by the energy working on your emotional body helping you to let go of the old ways that no longer serve you.
- Theta healing as I wrote earlier is a very effective way of changing belief systems.
- Working with your Angels. Especially Archangel Michael, he helps us to let go of what no longer serves us and gives us the strength and courage to move forward.

Many people ask me "How can I change another person"? Unfortunately you can't do this. People have free will, so the only person who can change them is them. It would be nice if we could re-program these people or at least help them to see things in a better light. So you either have to learn to let it go and love them for who they are or say a prayer for them that they will become open to other beliefs and live more in truth and love.

Remember it doesn't matter if you found your truths years ago or now. The fact is that you find it. Everyone finds their truths when it is the right time and they are ready emotionally, mentally and spiritually. We all see the light at some point. If you don't see yours yet, you will.

Affirmation: I now let go of old beliefs systems and live in my truths.
I always live with what makes my heart sing.

V—VISION BOARD

Vision Board: A visual of your goals, dreams and affirmations. As I have written throughout this book about being positive, attracting what you want, manifesting and so on. Vision boards are a great way of seeing your goals. Many people are very visual and need to see things right in front of them. This is a great way to do it. Not just for them but everyone who wants to manifest their dreams.

- Get your supplies: Poster Board (any size to fit your goals)

  - Pictures and/or photos
  - Magazines (For cutting out pictures)
  - Pens, pencils, markers, etc.
  - Glue, tape or photo tabs
  - Anything else you want to decorate your board.

Now think of what goals you want to achieve. Find pictures of these goals. For example if you were thinking of going back to school, get a picture of the school or a brochure and paste it on your board. Continue to put pictures on your board until all your goals are on there. Now if you have so many goals that you want to manifest, maybe start with the most important ones first then make another vision board later for the other goals. I feel that it is best to work with 5 or 6 goals to start.

Next write some affirmations on your board or find inspirational words in magazines that go with our goals and paste or write them on your board. You don't need long sentences; one-word affirmations are fine too. Here are some examples of positive words to use:

- Miracles
- Believe

- Abundance
- Prosperity
- Love
- Joy
- Gratitude
- Happiness
- Laugh
- Friends
- Family
- Positive
- Faith
- I Am

Or whatever else you can think of that pertains to what you want.

Then take time to decorate your vision board with stickers, artwork or whatever you want. Now put your vision board somewhere you will see it everyday. By doing this you can visualize your goals and stay positive knowing that you ARE achieving them.

Have fun making your vision board, don't rush through it because as you are making it you are placing your intentions into it. When I made mine I used a 12x12 scrap booking page and placed my goals on it with affirmations and decorations and placed it on my fridge and every time I walked by it I knew it was truth and knew it was on it's way. Now it is time for a new one because I have received everything on my board.

Don't be afraid to put really big goals on your board. Some times we feel that certain things are just out of reach and that is not true. Big things may just take a little longer to accomplish but you will accomplish them. Staying positive and acting as if you already have your goal is the biggest part. Keep your ego out of it. Again working from the heart will always get you through.

Here is a list of things you may want to attract into your life:

- New Job
- New Car
- New Home
- Pet
- Money
- Intuition

- Happiness
- Friends
- Relationship
- Health
- Vacation
- Any material objects
- Peace
- Or anything else you want

Get busy with those goals, dreams and desires and most of all have fun!!
"What you can believe, you can achieve"

W—WHAT, WHERE, WHEN & WHY

What do you want out of life? That is the BIG question. Take inventory of your life and see what needs to be changed, let go or attracted. Maybe you want or need materialistic things, and that is fine. If so then manifest it. Let go of the fear, release your ego and take what you have learned in this book and use it. Only you can decide to change, no one can do it for you. Changing takes work but it is well worth it. Remember you always have assistance from your guides, angels and of course God. Pay attention to the signs and messages you receive and follow it. All will be good!

Where do you start? In the beginning. Make a priority list of what you want or need to change, either in your head or on paper (Which I like better, can't forget that way). Then decide what is important in your life according to most to least with making sure you are on top of the list. Start with you and see if you are truly happy. If not then start down the list and see what needs to be done to achieve happiness. Start with the first thing and then move onto the next. Do one thing at a time and have patience because you will not change overnight. You have been the way you are for how long? It will take time but do not give up! Just being able to recognize that things in your life need changing is the first step. It is also showing that you are looking for a more positive way of life. So go for it!

When do you start? As soon as possible. Like I said as soon as you see that life is not what you want it to be, it is time to change. No if's, and's or but's. Don't let anyone tell you otherwise. You are in control of your life, no one else. Put your foot down and tell yourself that the time is NOW! Tell yourself "I AM GOING TO BE HAPPY NOW AND ALWAYS"!

Why? To be happier. To have more balance in your mind, body, soul and in your life. To live a life of love. To be more positive. To let go of what no longer serves you. To have positive supportive people in your life. To go with what you believe to be true in your heart. To have your own truths. To attract what you want. Because you want change and you say so!

Remember God put us all here to be HAPPY! So if you are not happy then get to work. Start with change, see what lessons you have learned, Let things go and always move forward!

X–X AMINING, X TEND AND X PRESS

X-amining your life. It is something we constantly do, even me. I have learned so much over the years, but I still have to check in every now and then to make sure I am balanced. There are times when I feel like things are off. So I look at my life and see what or who is not right in my life. Then I work at fixing or removing what is not needed and then just keep moving forward.

Schedule some time to re-X-amine your life. See if things are balanced and if not make some changes. Pay attention to what your body is telling you. Listen to the guidance and messages you receive. Follow through with what needs to be done. Remember to periodically check in with yourself. Especially when you are feeling off, blah or down in the dumps.

X-tend the love and positive attitude you have to everyone and in everything you do. The more we X-tend love, the more love grows within us and to others. X-tend what you have learned to those who may need it and are willing to listen. Help them to see a more positive way of life. When you see or hear negativity coming from someone, show them the positive way of things. We have to remember that with every negative there is a positive. We just need to open our eyes and hearts to see it. If they are not ready to hear it then let it go and they will change when they are ready. We can't change them, all we can do is pray for them and wish them well.

X-press your wants, needs and prayers to God, the angels, your guides and all those from the highest vibration of light. X-pect and know that help is there and prayers do get answered. They never let us down and always help us when asked.

X-press your love, feelings, thoughts and whatever may be on your mind to those around you. Keep the flow of communication going between you and your spouse, partner, friends and family. When things are not going well, X-press yourself. Holding stuff in will only make you unhappy and sick. If the other person doesn't know how you feel, it can't be fixed.

Y—YOGA

Y-Yoga, what is it? Yoga is built on three main structures: exercise, breathing, and meditation. The exercises of Yoga are designed to put pressure on the glandular systems of the body, increasing its efficiency and total health. The body is looked upon as the primary instrument that allows us to work and evolve in the world. Breathing techniques are based on the belief that breath is the source of life in the body. The Yoga student gently increases breath control to improve the health and function of both body and mind. These two systems of exercise and breathing then prepare the body and mind for meditation, and the student finds an easy approach to a quiet mind that allows silence and healing from everyday stress. Regular practice of all three parts of Yoga produces a clear, bright mind and a strong, able body.

There are over a hundred different types of Yoga. Some of the most well known are described below:

- Hatha Yoga: The physical movements and postures, plus breathing techniques. This is what most people associate with Yoga practice. Also good for beginners, Hatha typically requires a lot of breath work. Class is also likely to be focused on slow and gentle movements so it's a great type of yoga to wind down with at night.
- Vinyasa Yoga—Vinyasa is usually a fast-paced type of yoga with lots of different poses. Other than starting with a sun salutation, no two classes will be alike. You definitely won't get bored.
- Kundalini Yoga—"Kundalini" refers to the energy of the Root Chakra, which surrounds the area around your lower spine. Expect lots of work on your "core" area and your abs. You should also expect rapid movement and more sitting than usual.
- Kripalu Yoga—Considered to be one of the most gentle forms of yoga, Kripalu has more of an "inner focus." It's a great type of yoga

for those who are either out-of-shape or just beginning to practice, as you'll learn the basics in an easy manner.

- Restorative Yoga—Looking to wind down after a long day of work? Or perhaps you want to quiet your mind? Restorative yoga might be the answer as it's focused on relaxation.
- Prenatal Yoga—If you're an expectant mother then Prenatal yoga is probably for you. (Sorry, guys!) Some say that Prenatal is one of the best types of exercise for moms-to-be as there's a lot of core work and a focus on breathing.

Here at my center we offer Gentle (Hatha) Yoga and Vinyasa Yoga.

Yoga probably arrived in the United States in the late 1800s, but it did not become well known until the 1960s, as part of the youth culture's growing interest in anything Eastern. As more became known about the beneficial effects of Yoga, it gained acceptance and respect as a valuable method for helping in the management of stress and improving health and well-being. Many physicians now recommend Yoga practice to patients at risk for heart disease, as well as those with back pain, arthritis, depression, and other chronic conditions.

Yoga is not a religion. It has no creed or fixed set of beliefs, nor is there a prescribed godlike figure to be worshipped in a particular manner. Religions for the most part seem to be based upon the belief in and worship of things (God or godlike figures) that exist outside of oneself. The core of Yoga's philosophy is that everything is supplied from within an individual. Therefore there is no dependence on an any external figure, either in the sense of a person or god figure, or a religious organization. The practice of Yoga will not interfere with any religion. Many American Yoga Association students who have practiced Yoga for many years continue to follow the religious traditions they have grown up with or adopted without any issue.

Physiological Benefits of Yoga

- Stable autonomic nervous system equilibrium
- Pulse rate decreases
- Respiratory rate decreases
- Blood Pressure decreases (of special significance for hyporeactors)

- Galvanic Skin Response (GSR) increases
- EEG—alpha waves increase (theta, delta, and beta waves also increase during various stages of meditation)
- EMG activity decreases
- Cardiovascular efficiency increases
- Respiratory efficiency increases
- Gastrointestinal function normalizes
- Endocrine function normalizes
- Excretory functions improve
- Musculoskeletal flexibility and joint range of motion increase
- Breath-holding time increases
- Joint range of motion increase
- Grip strength increases
- Eye-hand coordination improves
- Dexterity skills improve
- Reaction time improves
- Posture improves
- Strength and resiliency increase
- Endurance increases
- Energy level increases
- Weight normalizes
- Sleep improves
- Immunity increases
- Pain decreases
- Steadiness improves
- Depth perception improves
- Balance improves
- Integrated functioning of body parts improves

Psychological Benefits of Yoga

- Somatic and kinesthetic awareness increase
- Mood improves and subjective well-being increases
- Self-acceptance and self-actualization increase
- Social adjustment increases
- Anxiety and Depression decrease
- Hostility decreases
- Concentration improves

- Memory improves
- Attention improves
- Learning efficiency improves
- Mood improves
- Self-actualization increase
- Social skills increases
- Well-being increases
- Somatic and kinesthetic awareness increase
- Self-acceptance increase
- Attention improves
- Concentration improves
- Memory improves
- Learning efficiency improves
- Symbol coding improves
- Depth perception improves
- Flicker fusion frequency improves

Biochemical Benefits of Yoga

- Glucose decreases
- Sodium decreases
- Total cholesterol decreases
- Triglycerides decrease
- HDL cholesterol increases
- LDL cholesterol decreases
- VLDL cholesterol decreases
- Cholinesterase increases
- Catecholamines decrease
- ATPase increases
- Hematocrit increases
- Hemoglobin increases
- Lymphocyte count increases
- Total white blood cell count decreases
- Thyroxin increases
- Vitamin C increases
- Total serum protein increases

Yoga Health Benefits versus Exercise Benefits

- **Yoga Benefits**

- Parasympathetic <u>Nervous System</u> dominates
- Subcortical regions of brain dominate
- Slow dynamic and static movements
- Normalization of muscle tone
- Low risk of injuring muscles and ligaments
- Low caloric consumption
- Effort is minimized, relaxed
- Energizing (breathing is natural or controlled)
- Balanced activity of opposing muscle groups
- Noncompetitive, process-oriented
- Awareness is internal (focus is on breath and the infinite)
- Limitless possibilities for growth in self-awareness

- **Exercise Benefits**

- Sympathetic Nervous System dominates
- Cortical regions of brain dominate
- Rapid forceful movements
- Increased muscle tension
- Higher risk of injury
- Moderate to high caloric consumption
- Effort is maximized
- Fatiguing (breathing is taxed)
- Imbalance activity of opposing groups
- Competitive, goal-oriented
- Awareness is external (focus is on reaching the toes, reaching the finish line, etc.)
- Boredom factor

Benefits taken from http://www.abc-of-yoga.com/beginnersguide/yogabenefits.asp

Z–ZIP TO IT!

Zip to it! Take what you have read throughout this book and start applying it to your life, one step at a time. Start small and work your way up. You will get there!

You may agree with everything I wrote about and you may not. My best advise is that you take what feels right to you and leave the rest behind. Go with what feels right in your heart, your heart will never steer you wrong. Give it a try; what have you got to lose?

Be patient with yourself as things will not change over night, but they will change. Be open to the possibilities. Be open to the guidance. Most of all be open to LOVE! Life is too short to hold onto the garbage of life. Stop and smell the flowers.

Affirmations

- I now change those things about me that no longer serve me!
- I am open for changes, for the better!
- I know that I deserve love and I accept it now
- Everything that is happening is only for the highest good of me.
- I trust that everything in my life is working for my highest good and I am receiving all that I am meant to have.
- On the soul level, I release all fear of failure.
- I replace indefinite, vague dreams with specific, detailed goals and action plans.
- Everything is working out for me now.

CPSIA information can be obtained at www.ICGtesting.com
Printed in the USA
BVOW060249240212

283698BV00001B/6/P